Columbia University
STUDIES IN ROMANCE PHILOLOGY AND LITERATURE

STAGE DECORATION IN FRANCE

IN THE MIDDLE AGES

STAGE DECORATION IN FRANCE

IN THE MIDDLE AGES

BY

DONALD CLIVE STUART, Ph.D.

AMS PRESS, INC.
NEW YORK
1966

NOTE

The following dissertation, having been examined by the Department of Romance Languages and Literatures of Columbia University, was considered to be a valuable contribution to the history of the medieval stage in France, and has been accepted in partial fulfilment of the requirement for the degree of Doctor of Philosophy.

HENRY ALFRED TODD.

COLUMBIA UNIVERSITY,
January, 1910.

TABLE OF CONTENTS

INTRODUCTION

CHAPTER I

CONCLUSION

INTRODUCTION

WRITERS on the subject of stage decoration in the Middle Ages have generally drawn their data from Religious plays alone. The question of the setting of the Profane stage has been left unsolved. The reason for this is that the mysteries and miracle plays are far more explicit in describing their scenery than are the farces and *sotties*. Also, after having reconstructed the simple decoration of the early liturgical drama, and after having mentioned the stage of the *Adam* play, investigators have then turned their attention to the great religious spectacles given in the open air in the fifteenth and sixteenth centuries, and have described at length the scenes and machines used in these really wonderful productions. An impression is left upon the mind of the reader that the typical stage of the Middle Ages was very large and contained many scenes, including Heaven, on a level above the stage, and a dragon's mouth representing Hell. But we shall attempt to prove that there were many other types of stages, ranging from the stage entirely without setting to the stage with many scenes on different levels. We shall try to show that no single kind of stage can be said to be typical of the Middle Ages to the exclusion of all others. The one characteristic common to the theaters of that period is that scenes were set simultaneously on the stage; but the number, the arrangement, the elaborateness varied greatly from time to time and from place to place. The stage of the *Actes des Apôtres* given in the amphitheater in Bourges must have presented a very different appearance from the stage of the same play given in the *Hôpital de la Trinité*. On the other hand, the *Farce du Cuvier* would not resemble the *Actes des Apôtres* in stage setting in the slightest degree, although they may have been represented on the same stage in Paris.

The division of the drama of the Middle Ages into the categories of religious and profane is convenient and has been followed in preparing this work. However, if the stage decoration of the religious drama alone is studied, and if the dramas of the fourteenth century are left out of consideration, as they have been, one cannot hope to arrive at the whole truth. Therefore the attempt has been made to reconstruct the setting of all kinds of drama at all times, as far as is possible; for only by considering the whole stage of the period can one finally gain a true impression of the system of stage decoration.

In order to fill the lacunæ in the history of stage setting, plays must be utilized which give little or even no hint of their scenery in stage directions, such as the *Miracles de Notre Dame* and practically all profane plays. How are we to gain information in regard to the setting of such plays, if stage directions are lacking? There is but one way: the lines themselves must furnish the desired evidence. This method, therefore, whether it be considered good or bad, must be accepted if one wishes to carry investigations of the subject farther than they have reached at present. The question must be decided whether these plays without stage directions were also without scenery; and if they had scenery, it must be reconstructed.

This method was suggested by the fact that in dramas whose stage setting is carefully described, the lines often anticipate the stage directions in the description of scenery. Then in turning to such plays as the *Miracles de Notre Dame,* which are almost entirely without stage directions, it is found that the lines contain constant references to scenery, and that the reader is rarely at a loss to know where the action is taking place. The question arises whether such references may not be wholly rhetorical. Yet this does not seem possible except in very few cases. No one can investigate this subject without being impressed by the fact that the stage carpenters—if we may thus apply a modern expression—were always striving after reality. Realism and reality are two underlying principles in the system of stage setting from the earliest plays down to the great mysteries. The simultaneous mounting of scenes is a proof of this. Thus, with this system in vogue, we cannot believe that when a character pointed out a window or knocked at a door and entered a house he carried on a mere pantomime in the empty air. There must have been scenery to correspond to such lines.

The author of the play no doubt intended his text to be followed in setting the scenes.

Direct proof of this is found in a stage direction of the *Mistère du Vieil Testament*. In one passage the angels are told to show themselves in the order *comme dit le texte*. Later there is a direct reference to scenery itself which is to be *ordonnez selon le texte*. Because of the above considerations this method has been employed not only when stage directions are lacking; but evidence furnished by the lines has also been used to complete evidence furnished by the directions. It is by this means that we hope to prove that more than two levels were used on the stage in order to make the scenery more realistic; that the interior of Hell was often visible; that the dragon's head was not as frequent a setting for Hell as has been supposed; that stages were also common on which very few scenes appeared.

It is not claimed that this method is entirely successful and accurate for all plays. At times doubts arise as to whether a certain scene, vaguely mentioned by the lines, appeared upon the stage at all; and, if it did appear, whether it was carefully set or merely indicated. For example, it is sometimes hard to decide whether a provost or judge sat in a chair representing

his house, or whether a special setting was used
for the scene.   Yet these questions arise quite
rarely, and they do not affect the evidence as a
whole.   In each case when the doubtful scene
occurs, attention has been called to the fact that
it is doubtful; but plays in which such scenes
arise have been avoided as much as possible.
Thus, while there may be a difference of opinion
in regard to the problematical existence on the
stage of one or two scenes in some plays, especially in the longer miracle plays, the lines are
to be depended upon, as a rule, to a degree that
may hardly seem possible to one who has not
tested this method.

As far as has been practicable the plays have
been treated separately, since it has been our
purpose to show the many different kinds of
settings that existed in the Middle Ages.   A
description of a scene in Heaven or in Hell
drawn from the stage directions of all the great
mysteries would tend to magnify the relative
importance of these scenes on the whole medieval stage.   There is no doubt that these two
scenes were often set with special care, and the
eyes of the spectator must have seen many novel
effects in them; but the stages must not be left

out of the account upon which these scenes were
not set at all, or if they were set, did not by
any means constitute the all-enthralling scenes,
since little action took place in them.   Also,
more attention has been given to the settings
themselves than to the wonderful machinery
employed by the producers of the open air
mysteries.

In regard to the brief treatment of the question of the origin of medieval drama, let it be
said that we realize that the belief in an unbroken dramatic tradition rests upon theory
more than upon facts.   The lack of written
dramas in the period in which some believe the
tradition to have been broken means very little,
for drama, according to the broad definition
which must be given it when such questions
arise, can easily exist without the written word.
There may have been no texts in this period of
dramatic history; but since we find no extant
texts, either because none existed or because all
were lost, are we to believe that the dramatic
concept ceased to exist?   The evidence of texts
would be gratifying, but the want of such evidence does not induce us to believe in a rebirth
of drama.   Such a phenomenon is more diffi-

cult to accept than the phenomenon, so easily explained, of the lack of evidence of the existence of a form of art during a hundred years at a time when confusion reigned, and when this particular form of art was more or less under the ban of the law. One might be more skeptical if it were a question of any real literary form. But drama is not inherently a literary form of art. It does not even need to be spoken, in order to exist and to live.

However, in regard to this problem and all others discussed in the following pages, it has been our aim to be undogmatic. The study was undertaken not in the hope of overthrowing existing theories, but in order to cast new light upon the subject by the investigation of dramas by means of a method hitherto unemployed as far as this period is concerned. Finally, the work seemed worth while in order to present the setting of the whole medieval stage in France, and not merely a part of it as has been done heretofore, for only by studying the whole stage can one understand the real condition of the stage decoration of the Middle Ages.

It is to be regretted that, owing to the necessity of frequent citations from medieval plays, the text of the present volume must change so often from English to Old French; but it has seemed inadvisable to translate passages from which data are drawn for such a work as this. The word *maison,* which is used in rather a technical sense and which is untranslatable in this special use, may need explanation. It means either a piece of scenery, or a scene itself. Thus a setting may consist of six *maisons* or scenes, one of which may, for example, be a mountain. It is also used with the meaning of "house," in the sense that the house is represented by real scenery and not merely by a chair.

In view of the fact that the necessary bibliographical indications have been given in connection with all references throughout the book, it has been thought that no general bibliography is here called for. A sufficient index to the various subjects treated will be found conveniently provided in the analytical table of contents prefixed to the volume.

It is with deep gratitude that the author expresses his thanks to Professor H. A. Todd, who suggested this subject for investigation and under whose kind and scholarly supervision the work has been carried on.

CHAPTER I

The Question of an Uninterrupted Dramatic Tradition. Earliest Records of Scenery. A possible Origin of the Use of Chairs as Scenery. Introduction of Real Scenery. The *Sponsus*. Heaven not Represented in Early Plays. The Stage on One Level.

THE drama of the Middle Ages has been divided into two kinds: religious and profane. There is no exact line of demarcation between them, since the religious and profane elements are early mingled on the stage. Yet it has been found expedient by authors to treat these two forms of dramatic representation not only in separate chapters of the same book but even in different books. The result of this practice has been to establish two statements in regard to the origin of drama. It is generally accepted that the profane or comic theater is a direct outgrowth of the mime. The religious theater is supposed to find its beginning in Christian worship. Professor Petit de Julleville goes so far as to say that religion created the drama, and he draws the oft-repeated parallel between the origin of the drama in Greece and in France.[1]

The definition of drama, as far as the Middle Ages are concerned, must be made very broad. It must include almost any attempt to represent an historical or imaginary event either by tableaux, pantomime, or dialogue spoken or sung. Therefore if the mime used any of these means of entertainment and thus preserved the spark of comedy, the theory of a second birth of the drama in Europe must be given up. If the mime consisted of only dances and rope-walking in the eighth and ninth centuries, when we last hear of it in France before the rise of liturgical drama, it is difficult to explain why the church was so hostile to this harmless form of entertainment. Reich is of the opinion that the dramatic mime lived throughout the Middle Ages, and he gives citations of authors who refer to mimes as late as the year 836.[2] The primitive drama of the adoration of the shepherds was played in the tenth century.[3] Since

---

[1] Les Mystères, Paris, 1880, vol. I. p. 2.

[2] Der Mimus, Berlin, 1903, ch. 9.

[3] Petit de Julleville, les Mystères, vol. I, p. 25.

836 is by no means the date of the passing of
the mimes, and since they are considered important enough to be mentioned by Agobert, it
is probable that their art lived at least until
the liturgical drama began.   Then the liturgical drama would be a religious mime.   It is
difficult to believe that the profane dramatic
representations did not give the impulse to these
religious representations.   Is it not possible
that even before there were tropes interpolated
into the services, there were mimed representations of sacred events?   Du Méril[4] brings evidence that this was the case.   He quotes Fridegod
as saying in 956 of Saint Ouen, who lived in the
seventh century: In eorum domo non ut assolet
in quorundam saeculorum conviviis mimorum
vel histrionum carmina foeda sed evangelica vel
apostolica sive prophetica personabant oracula.
Whether this is true of Saint Ouen or not, at
least it is evidence that early in the tenth century there was a tradition of the representation of sacred *oracula* at a time when *mimi* and
histriones still existed.   If this is true of the
seventh century, then there was a kind of

4 Origines latines du théâtre moderne, Paris, 1849.

drama before the appearance of tropes. In either case there is the probability that mimes and a kind of religious drama were contemporaneous.

That the profane mime was popular with all classes of people is sufficiently attested by the fulminations of the church against it. Some form of drama is dear to the hearts of all peoples. The churchmen seem to have had little success in putting a stop to plays up to 836 at least. From the tenth century on, dramatic representations flourish. Is it possible that for the space of a hundred years, at the most, the interest in such shows was dead after having been so hard to kill before this time, and living so strongly afterward?

Taking this evidence into consideration, it seems that the theory as to the origin of French drama should be modified. Dramas with a religious subject are born in the church, of Christian worship. But the spirit of drama was kept in the mimes at least until the liturgical drama furnished the people with representations which took the place of the mimes. Therefore drama did not die; but was handed down in crude forms, at times, until the present day.[5]

Where, then, in the history of stage decoration, should investigations begin? The setting of the stage should be traced from the earliest Roman plays and spectacles through the Middle Ages. Unfortunately documents giving information as to the exact nature of the mimes in France are lacking. It is impossible, at the present time, to describe the state of the scenery which was in vogue when the first liturgical plays were acted. Yet, because scenery plays an important part throughout the Middle Ages, and because scenery is carefully indicated in the early liturgical drama, it seems probable that it was never wholly neglected, especially if the character of the representation were such that a setting of some kind would have aided in making the dialogue or action clearer to the spectator. There is little reason for doubting, however, that whatever scenery was displayed, was improvised.

[5] Reich has reached the same conclusion by using somewhat different data, *op. cit.*, p. 854, note 1. His comparison between the mime and the mystery, which is a much later development, is not very strong evidence. Such parallels are too easily made.

The use of chairs to represent different local-
ities is a characteristic of what may be called
the stage of the liturgical drama.   Is this the
invention of some scribe who wrote one of these
dramas, and was this convention then accepted
for all times after the representation in which it
first occurred; or is it an outgrowth of the
"stage" of *histriones* or mimes?   It would be
natural, when these actors, if they may be dignified with that name, came to the hall of some
seigneur, to clear a space for them.   There
would be no "behind the scenes"; but if one
of them was not engaged in the show during a
certain time he would probably sit down, in
order not to attract attention away from the
performer, as was done throughout the Middle
Ages.   Just as to-day, chairs would be placed
for them.   If there was a trace of drama in
these shows, and if it was necessary to the action
that one character should come from a certain
place or go to a character who was supposed to
be in another locality, in the minds of the spectators the chair from which he came or the
chair in which the second character was sitting,
would represent that locality, be it house, town,
or country.   The next step, the formal repre-

sentation of a room or house by a chair, would be made easily. It seems possible, therefore, that the custom of placing chairs or seats of some kind on the stage to be occupied by performers when not acting, and the convention of having chairs represent scenes, come from such performances, which antedate the liturgical drama.

The first indications of scenery occur in the liturgical drama. It is striking that the directions for the setting and for the action are so carefully noted. The spectacle is at least as important as the lines, if not more so. The *Planctus Mariæ et aliorum*[6] is remarkable in that each line is accompanied by a direction for the action. The element of pantomime is so strong in this play that it seems possible that there may have been religious mimes to which lines to be sung were added later, and that the liturgical drama is not an outgrowth of tropes but of sacred pantomimes. This drama, which was in effect a pantomime, belongs probably to the thirteenth century; but in the *Trois Rois*,[7]

[6] Coussemaker, Drames liturgiques, Didron, 1861. P. 285.

[7] *Ibid.* p. 242.

which is one of the most primitive forms of
liturgical drama, pantomime is found.   A
Cantor explains the action: *Magi veniunt ab
Oriente.* For the moment the play becomes in
reality a sacred pantomime. Taking into consideration the importance of spectacle and action it does not seem too bold to conjecture that
religious mimes, not tropes without scenery,
are the primitive form of liturgical drama.
Nor is it strange if no descriptions or directions
for such representations have been preserved.
The action could be easily improvised in a
moment. Only when words and music were
combined with it, would it seem necessary and
important that the play should be intrusted to
writing. Thus the early tropes of the tenth
century would be naturally preserved. But is
it certain that these early forms of antiphonal
service were unaccompanied by action? Or,
when the *Quem quæritis in præsepe, pastores,
dicite* was sung, was there a kind of pantomime
going on before the altar, which then represented the *præsepe* in some way, as it did later?
In this case the tropes would bear the same rela-
tion to the action as the words sung by the
Cantor in the *Trois Rois.* They would be the

2

explanation and accompaniment of the drama. Undoubtedly the idea of dialogue developed from the tropes; but it is possible that the action existed before the dialogue. Even if it be granted that the tropes grew up independently of any action, it is still more natural to believe that the action was introduced into the Church from profane dramatic representations: the same representations, whatever they were, which kept comedy alive. The tropes would then be considered as merely a part of the worship; but when they are combined with or are sung in accompaniment to action, the liturgical drama exists.

Action and spectacle, in a crude way, are so important that it is difficult to believe that they sprung and developed so quickly from tropes.[8] One naturally seeks the origin of drama in such action and mimicry. Dialogue is rather an outgrowth than an inherent necessity. For these reasons and those cited above, it does not seem possible that the drama of the Middle Ages was born in the Church and that its primitive form

[8] See the formula used in England in the tenth century where the action is so important. Lange, Die lateinischen Osterfeiern, München, 1887, p. 38.

was the trope. On the contrary, the most important element of the drama, action or mimicry, seems to have lived in mimes at least until it was introduced into the worship of the Church, which lends itself to action so readily. There is evidence which points to religious pantomime. The next step would be the explanation of this pantomime by a *Cantor* or by tropes. The combination of tropes and action formed the liturgical drama.

The occasions on which the worship lent itself to mimetic action are many. The dedication of a church with the ritual of Gallican origin,[9] and the worship during holy week, are striking examples. Since such actions existed before the writing of tropes, and since the liturgical drama grew up soon after the interpolation of such dialogue, the question may be raised again as to whether the tropes were unaccompanied by action. The difference between a trope and liturgical drama seems to lie in the fact that the manuscript of the latter contains the directions for action. Is it not possible that the earliest form of the *Quem quæritis*

[9] Chambers, Mediæval Stage, Oxford, 1903, vol. II, pp. 4, 5.

of the St. Gall manuscript was accompanied by action—action which was taken for granted and not described? In the eleventh century trope of St. Martial of Limoges a narrative passage is found. This is a parallel to the *Trois Rois* in which the narrative element exists. A most striking bit of evidence that action is the most important part of liturgical drama is found in the *Concordia Regularis* of St. Ethelwold[10] drawn up before the close of the twelfth century. The action is described very minutely in narrative form. Songs to be sung are indicated, and the dialogue is mentioned. It is the action, however, which is most carefully described. The existence of a liturgical drama in this form points to action accompanying the earliest tropes. This formula seems to be an example of the primitive way of preserving a liturgical drama. It is not necessarily the most primitive form of drama. It does not seem probable that an action so developed could have been suggested by tropes alone. The tropes are rather an addition to mimetic action, which, in itself, is drama, for drama can exist without dialogue.

[10] Chambers, *op. cit.*, vol. II, p. 14.

For these reasons it is misleading to consider that there was a second birth of drama in Europe. The profane mime, if it kept comedy alive, must have action or dialogue or both. At least, such drama seems to have existed until the religious mimetic action arose. The idea of drama is therefore best considered as merely transferred from the profane to the religious subject. The form of Christian worship fostered dramatic representations of a religious nature. The profane element which exists in some of the earliest extant liturgical plays is, in itself, evidence of profane representations the account of which is lost to us.

The earliest references to scenery point to the altar as stage and setting. A sepulchre is " made in a vacant part of the altar and a veil stretched on a ring" covers it until the adoration of the cross is over in the *Concordia Regularis*. Chambers believes that this sepulchre is made on the altar by the " laying together of some of the silver service-books," as was done at Narbonne several centuries later.[11] Since the cross which is laid in it is small enough to be held on a cushion, the sepulchre itself was

[11] *Op. cit.*, p. 17, note 1; p. 21.

probably small.   Even in this drama a chair is
used, although it cannot be regarded as part of
the scenery.   After having kissed the cross the
abbot is directed to go *ad sedem suam.*   It may
be that the use of chairs as scenery originated
from such customs, rather than in the manner
indicated above.

The representation of the sepulchre became
more elaborate.   In the *Nuit de Pâques*[12] the
sepulchre can be opened and entered.   That the
sepulchre is not the altar is shown by the fact
that they are both mentioned as different places
by the stage direction: *Hoc dicto, Marie exeant
de sepulchro; post appareat Dominus in sinistro
cornu altaris.*   This may have been scenery
made specially, or a curtained recess such as
served for the sepulchre.   The crypt also served
as scenery for the sepulchre, as in the drama of
the text of Würzburg,[13] where the angels descend into the crypt to await the coming of the
three Marys.

The drama of the *Trois Rois* shows a primitive form of setting for the plays given at
Christmas.   The star is shown, and a part of

---

[12] Coussemaker, Drames liturgiques, p. 250.
[13] Lange, Die lateinischen Osterfeiern, p. 53.

the altar is concealed by curtains which, when drawn back, disclose the child. The angel does not appear to have been in some high place as if speaking from Heaven. The direction reads . . . *quidam Puer, alba indutus, quasi Angelus, antiphonam ante altare illis dicat.* The *Office des Pasteurs,*[14] played at Rouen, directs that the scene be set as follows: *Præsepe sit paratum retro altare et imago sanctæ Mariæ sit in eo posita.* In this play the angels are in an elevated place. In the *Adoration des Mages*[15] they are supposed to appear *in excelsis.* At times, the boy representing the angel was placed *super pulpitum.*[16] Such arrangements are the beginnings from which the representation of Heaven above the stage grew. But such settings are not to be considered as a real representation of Heaven. Even the effect of a two-storied stage does not exist. There are voices speaking from on high. There is no evidence of scenery. The decoration of Heaven is not a characteristic of the liturgical drama but of the later Passion play. The indefinite *in excelsis* and *alto loco* are evidence that the scene was not set.

[14] Du Méril, p. 147.
[15] Du Méril, p. 162.
[16] Du Méril, p. 99.

The *Massacre des innocents*[17] demands a more complicated setting. Besides the *præsepe* and the angel speaking *ab excelso,* Herod is found seated on a throne as is shown in both directions and lines. Egypt and Galilee are mentioned, but were probably without designation. It is always a question as to whether such places were marked with scenery. It seems, however, that the *partem Galilee* would be the place from which Joseph went, and that the spectators would understand. The *Adoration des Mages* illustrates how such action was carried on without scenery in the following direction: *Interim Magi prodeuntes, quisque de angulo suo quasi de regione sua.* The spectator was supposed to know from whence they came. Such a place was practically behind the scenes. Even though a character was in view of the audience at all times, he could be imagined as coming from any place. He was, in effect, behind the scenes until his part began.

Another convention which is found in the liturgical drama and which exists throughout the Middle Ages is that each actor has a special place to which he goes when not actively en-

[17] Coussemaker, p. 166.

gaged in the performance. In the drama of *le Sépulchre*,[18] for example, the actors are directed to go *ad locum suum*. This was evidently a means of keeping order on the stage. If a character was important and had a *maison* or chair, he returned to it. If not, he probably went to a place where he would be out of the way.

The *Conversion de Saint Paul*[19] shows a distinct advance in the art of stage setting. The direction reads as follows: *Ad representandam Conversionem beati Pauli apostoli, paretur in competenti loco, quasi Jerusalem, quedam sedes, et super eam Princeps sacerdotum. Paretur et alia sedes, et super eam juvenis quidam in similitudine Sauli; habeatque secum ministros armatos. Ex alia vero parte, aliquantulum longe ab his sedibus, sint parate quasi in Damasco due sedes; in altera quarum sedeat vir quidam nomine Judas, et in altera Princeps Synagoge Damasci. Et inter has duas sedes sit paratus lectus, in quo jaceat vir quidam in similitudine Ananie.* Thus chairs instead of real scenery are used to represent cities; but is there in this

[18] Coussemaker, p. 298.
[19] Coussemaker, p. 210.

play a simple piece of scenery in the shape of a wall, as Cohen interprets the direction:[20] ... *in sporta ab aliquo alto loco, quasi a muro. . . . ?* This hardly points to a special scene constructed for the purpose.

Real scenery, however, makes its appearance in the *Résurrection de Lazare.*[21] The house of Simon is mentioned, and it could not be a chair since a table is set in it. *Tunc Simon inducat Jesum in domum suam, et, posita mensa. . . .* Later in the play the house is mentioned in the following direction: "However let the house of Simon, when he himself has gone, be treated as if Bethany." If the rest of the play is read, it is seen that Bethany means the house of Mary and Martha. Lazarus falls sick in it and lies *in lectulo.* There is also a direction: *Maria tacite a domo egrediente.* Had there been no scenery for the house itself when it belonged to Simon, but merely a table, or when it belonged to Mary and Martha had there been merely a bed, it would not have been so carefully directed that the space be considered as Mary's and Martha's house. There must have

[20] Cohen, Histoire de la mise-en-scène, Paris, 1906, p. 25.
[21] Coussemaker, p. 221.

been a setting for the house. Thus *maisons* and real scenery are found even in liturgical drama.

The direction to use the same scenery twice in one play is significant. It is the means of keeping down the number of *maisons* when the space is limited. Since, as a general rule, the stage business of the simple liturgical drama differs little from that of the larger and more complicated plays, it may be inferred that this natural way of re-using scenery was employed later whenever it was necessary to reduce the number of *maisons,* as for example in some of the *Miracles de Notre Dame* which were given indoors.

In the *Fils de Gédron*[22] the scenery is still more complicated. The directions call for a throne, *Rex Marmorinus in alta sede;* the church of St. Nicholas which can be entered, *ad ecclesiam Sancti Nicolai eant; in quam cum introierint;*—and also the house of Euphrosina into which she enters and sets a table, *eat in domum suam, et paret mensam.* The doors of this house are mentioned both in the directions and the lines. Such direct references to scenery can hardly be rhetorical. This drama, with its set-

[22] Coussemaker, p. 123.

ting, together with the *Daniel* from the MS. of Beauvais, foreshadows the later miracle plays. The *Daniel* did not form an integral part of the worship. The scenery consisted of a throne and at least one wall of the palace, on which a hand wrote the fateful words. The lion's den was shown and its interior was visible. These are simple settings, but they prove that scenery was employed in the early liturgical drama in about the same manner as in the later mysteries.

The drama of the *Sponsus*,[23] generally dated as belonging to the eleventh century, shows a developed form of liturgical drama. The text is no longer entirely in Latin. The element of spectacle has begun to increase in importance at the expense of the element of worship. Hell was represented. Demons were introduced, one is tempted to say, for the delectation of the audience. There is little difference, in spirit and effect, between the scene implied in the direction: *Modo accipiant eas et precipitentur in infernum,* and the *diablerie* in any later mystery. This play was acted in a church; but it does not contain more religious elements than

[23] Monmerqué et Michel, Théâtre français au moyen âge, Paris, 1842.

are found in the *Miracles de Notre Dame,* which
hardly ought to be classed as religious drama.
There is only one sacred character in the *Sponsus,* while the virgins, the merchants and especially the devils are profane. They are not con-
nected with any religious festival as the shepherds are with Christmas. The lines were
sung; but the effect of the play and the interest
it aroused must have differed from the effect
and interest aroused by the antiphonal lines of
a purely religious drama sung at Easter or
Christmas. Thus as early as the eleventh century, granted that the *Sponsus* is not anterior
to the year 1000,[24] the drama has already
reached a stage of development which is not
wholly religious and entirely wrapped up with
the ritual.

Petit de Julleville has described the scenery
of this play. He believed that Hell was represented by "*un gouffre d'où s'échappaient des
flammes.* Also, since there was a Hell, he was
of the opinion that Heaven was represented
above the place where the merchants stood.
However, if the lines are read and the implied
action is considered, a different conclusion is

[24] Les Mystères, vol. 1, p. 27.

reached. The wise and foolish virgins are at first together. The foolish virgins are told to go and buy oil of two merchants who "stand there."[25] They go and return, but cry out: *Aperire fac nobis ostium.* This line shows a door to the place they had left, which was not Heaven, but is referred to by the *Sponsus* as: *Hujus aule limine.* It is more of a terrestrial paradise or sacred court. It was probably represented by some inclosure, and it may have been the place about the altar with a gate.

Heaven is not mentioned or needed. As to the scenery which represented Hell, one is reduced to conjecture. It may have been the crypt which served for this scene. As for flames issuing from Hell, there is no reason for believing that the scene was so realistic. The mere representation of Hell is an isolated case in extant liturgical dramas; and such realism in scenery is more characteristic of later mysteries produced in the open air.

This play and its setting show a development in liturgical drama. Its date is therefore important in regard to the growth of liturgical drama, the birth of which Petit de Julleville

[25] *Que lai veet ester.*

places somewhat after the year 1000. But there is reason to believe that the *Sponsus* may have been composed even before this date. The play deals with the coming of Christ and warns people to be ready for him. This is a natural subject to deal with just before or perhaps during the year 1000 when the return of Christ was expected. Such a play would probably be written before rather than after this date. Thus if there is comparatively developed liturgical drama at the end of the tenth century, the date of the rise of purely religious drama must be put back. The gap between the last remnants of Latin dramatic representations and liturgical drama is lessened. The presence of dramatic action and scenery in the state in which they are found in the *Sponsus* at such a date is evidence that the spirit of drama never died, but that the actors and authors of religious drama took their cue from profane dramatic action.

The development of the setting of the liturgical drama may be summed up as follows. The setting began at the altar, but moved away from it as other scenes were needed. Both chairs and *maisons* were used to represent places, all of which are generally represented at once, although a *maison* may represent two places successively. The scenery is comparatively exact, the rule being that what is necessary to the action is represented. These are about the same conditions as will prevail throughout the Middle Ages. There is however this difference. Hell does not play an important part in liturgical drama. Heaven can hardly be said to have been represented at all. There have been angels in high places as *aux voûtes de l'église;* but these references are to the sky from which the angels make the annunciation or hover over the manger, and they do not give evidence that the place where the angels were was decorated to represent Heaven. The setting of the liturgical drama does not give the effect of a two-storied stage, but of a stage of one level. It is true that the custom of representing Heaven above the level of the stage proper grew from the custom of having angels in *alto loco,* etc.; but this is a later development.

CHAPTER II

The Thirteenth Century Setting of the *Adam* Play.
Résurrection du Sauveur Probably on One Level. Early
Profane Drama.

THE withdrawal of the stage from the altar
to the public square was accomplished even by
liturgical dramas. Thus it is not surprising to
find the mystery play of *Adam* given in front
of the church in the thirteenth[1] century. The
Latin stage directions which accompany this
play are copious and, it is to be believed, exact.
The direction *manu monstrabit portas ecclesie*
is evidence that the scene was set in front of
a church. The raised space, to which a few
steps lead, found before the doors of many
churches, would have sufficed easily for the
needs of this play, and from such a stage the
devils could make the directed *discursum per
populum*. There is no evidence of a scaffolding being built for the stage; and if the space

[1] Paul Meyer, Romania, 1903, p. 637. Luzarche,
Adam, Tours, 1854.

in front of the church were not raised, it is possible that there was no stage constructed, but that actors and spectators were on the same level, as they probably were when a play was given within a church.

As for the setting, Terrestrial Paradise is probably placed above the level of the rest of the stage, although the direction: *Constituatur paradisus loco eminenciori* may mean that the scene is merely to be prominent. There are curtains around it so that the actors within are only visible from the shoulders up. There are also sweet-smelling flowers and trees, including the Tree of Life. This scene is not to be mistaken for Heaven—a place which was not shown in early dramas as it is in the later plays. Heaven is only represented figuratively by the church, into which the actor impersonating God is directed to enter when his presence on the stage is not necessary. This scene is quite different from the later stages, which were dominated by God and the angels sitting on high. What this disposition of scenery does show, is the· ever-present realism of the stage in the Middle Ages. Paradise is better than earth, and hence is usually shown on a higher plane.

Hell was also represented. It is impossible to determine its locality and level. Its interior was probably not visible since there is nothing to indicate a scene in Hell. Smoke escapes from it and an infernal din is heard from within. It can be entered, but the scenery serving for this entrance is merely described as *portas inferni.* Thus gates or doors from which smoke escapes may be accounted all the scenery of Hell. Had there been more, the author, so exact and minute in his other directions and descriptions, would have noted the details; but this scene appears to be unimportant in regard to construction, although the devils play a large rôle in the action.

The setting for the rest of the stage is simple. Thorns and tares spring up in the ground cultivated by Adam. Two large stones serve for the altars of Cain and Abel. The place where the murder is committed is designated as *locum remotum quasi secretum,* but, so far as appears, there was no special scenery. The only properties for those who prophesy the coming of Christ are a throne or seat where each remains while he speaks his lines before being carried into Hell. Nothing else is needed. Thus while this stage must have been very simple in regard to setting, a distinct advance is noted beyond the scenery of the purely liturgical drama.

The fragment of the *Résurrection du Sauveur*[1a] of the thirteenth century shows a setting, indicated by the prologue, which points to one level. The crucifix, the tomb, and a jail are to be made ready first. The following lines refer to Heaven and Hell:

> Enfer seit mis de cele part,
> Es mansions de l'altre part,
> E puis le ciel;

If these lines are to be trusted, the conclusion will be reached that neither was Heaven above the rest of the stage nor was Hell below it. This would be the natural interpretation of the passage, while to conclude that Heaven was above in this setting is to interpret the passage in terms of the stage in the fourteenth and fifteenth centuries. Although the *Adam* play may show the beginning of the two-storied stage, yet the usual stage of the early plays is on one level, and there is nothing to show that the setting

[1a] Monmerqué et Michel, *op. cit.*

of this *Résurrection* departed from this custom.
If the play was produced at all, it may have
been inconvenient to build a two-storied stage,
especially if it was given in a church. Even
though a reference in a play of this period might
be found which would give proof of a scene in
Heaven above the stage, it would still seem that
the author of this fragment had followed the
stage setting of the liturgical drama, perhaps
because he had seen no other style of setting or
possibly for reasons of convenience.

Galilee is supposed to be *en mi la place.* It
is a question whether there was any scenery to
mark the place. One is inclined to believe that
the location of the country is being pointed out
by the person who recited the prologue; and
that there was no particular scene, as was the
case in the *Massacre des innocents,* when the
three kings went " just as if from their own
kingdom." The house at Emmaus is shown,
however; but there are merely seats for Pilate,
Caiaphas, Joseph of Arimathea, Nicodemus,
the Jews, the disciples, the three Marys.
Whether the retainers sat or stood about Pilate
is not clear. At any rate the number of scenes
is very small, Heaven, Hell, the jail, the house

at Emmaus, the cross, and the tomb being the
real scenery, and probably all on one level.

The scenery of the *Jeu de Saint Nicolas*,[2]
written by Jean Bodel early in the thirteenth
century, was surely placed on one elevation, since
neither Heaven nor Hell was represented.
Whether the angel who appeared to the army
was above it or not, is of little consequence.
All information in regard to the appearance of
the stage of this play must be gained from the
lines alone. Petit de Julleville claims to have
noted thirty-eight changes of the place of action; but this has nothing to do with the amount
of scenery used.

One of the most important scenes is in the
palace of the king, where the king naturally
would be seated on a throne. The idol Tervagan
is seen in the palace; but it was represented by
a living actor since it speaks. Later the treasure is exposed, probably within the same
scenery. An image of Saint Nicholas rests
upon the treasure. The interior and the exterior of a prison were also necessary to the
action. As for the tavern, an exterior was
surely visible. Thus there were three *maisons,*

---

[2] Monmerqué et Michel, *op. cit.*

but there was probably no special setting to
mark the houses of the emirs, who are merely
summoned from their place on the stage in
very short scenes. Also the two camps of the
armies and the battlefield would not require a
setting. The prologue gives evidence of a hut
or cabin when it speaks of the worthy man who
is found *en une manoque*. Thus the stage may
be conceived as set with four pieces of scenery:
the palace, prison, tavern, and hut, all of which
probably showed both an interior and an
exterior.

The *Miracle de Théophile* by Rutebeuf presents difficulties which make it impossible to
reconstruct the exact number of scenes used.
Even if the rule be applied that scenery which
is necessary to the action was shown, yet the
lines are in some cases rather obscure. That
the stage was decorated by at least one *maison*
is proved by the direction: *Ici se repent Théo-
philes et vient à une chapele de Nostre Dame.*
The line *Vez ci vostre ostel et le mien* points
to a second *maison* used as the bishop's house.
This may have been merely a chair; but as a
general rule scenery was used for the house of
a person who was important to the action and

before or within whose house or palace much of
the action took place.   The custom being to set
the stage with several *maisons,* it would be
natural to use scenery for the house of the
bishop, especially at this period in the development of stage setting, when realism was growing.

Whether the sorcerer had a separate house
or not is an open question.   The conjuring up
of Satan was evidently a scene designed to
interest the eyes of the spectators, but it is
difficult to decide whether that interest was
augmented by the use of scenery.   Also the
place that Satan occupied on the stage is referred to by Notre Dame in the line: *Sathan,*
Sathan, es tu en serre?   This may be a mere
summoning, or it may have been a scene representing Hell in a way.   But since the lines are
so indefinite in this play, it may be assumed
that there was no spectacular scene in Hell
such as is found on the stage two hundred years
later.   The stage in any case showed few
scenes, whether this conjectured scenery appeared or not.   It is again to be noted that
Heaven is not represented.

The profane stage at this period evidently

did not differ greatly in appearance from the
stage of these semi-religious plays, if the evidence gained from the plays of Adam de la
Hale may be trusted. Again the setting must
be reconstructed from the lines; but as Petit
de Julleville says, these plays " demand always
action and stage setting." A bower of foliage
is constructed in the *Jeu de la Feuillée* when
the fairies enter; and a table is set before a
tavern and the interior is implied in the line:
Oue, il est chaiens. As for the Wheel of Fortune, there is no doubt but that it was visible,
otherwise the lines referring to it would be in-
comprehensible to the spectators, and they are
far too vivid not to apply to a real piece of
scenery.

Robin et Marion, produced first before the
court of Naples in 1283 and later in France,
demands a pastoral scene with bushes and
flowers, there being many direct references to
such scenery. There is also one reference to
the door of a *maison* in *Ouvrez-moi tost l'uis.*
The phrase *Vers ceste riviere* also implies
scenery, although the river was not necessary
to the action and may have been behind the
scenes. At any rate, the stage of these two

plays was set in a simple manner, while the
Jeu du Pèlerin does not require any setting.

The only other profane play of this period is
the early form of the farce of the *Garçon et
l'Aveugle*,[3] dated between 1266 and 1290. The
action of the play needs one scene representing the house of the *Aveugle*. The lines read
as follows:

> Je vorroie ore estre en maison;
> Quant tu viens à .j. grant perron
> Deus maisons de là siet mes més.

The two characters arrive before the house,
and the Garçon says:

> Sire, je i sui, or vous souffrés,
> Jou verrai l'uis où siet le clinkes.

The *Aveugle* replies:

> Hannet, une fuelle de venke
> A sor le suell où elle siet.

All this might be rhetorical were it not for the
fact that the house is entered—*Sire, ens estes*—
and the blind man is left there by the boy. As
soon as a piece of scenery is necessary to the

[3] Paul Meyer, Jahrbuch für romanische und englische
Litteratur, vol. 6, p. 163.

action, one may be reasonably sure that it was represented.

The stage of the thirteenth century was by no means complicated. Admitting all possible scenes, the number of *maisons* was small. The scenery itself appears to have been exact but not elaborate in comparison with what it will become later. The scene in Hell plays an insignificant part, if the extant plays may be taken as examples of a general rule. The *Adam* play may show a double elevation for the stage; but a two-storied stage with a decorated scene in Heaven can hardly be regarded as the characteristic setting of the period. At least the majority of the stages seem to have been set on one level; and though a two-storied stage may have existed at this time, it is not the only type.

CHAPTER III

Tableaux and Pantomimes. Great Variety of Scenes.
Use of Different Levels. Setting of an Early Provençal
Play. Influence of the Tableaux and Pantomimes.

TEXTS belonging to the first half of the fourteenth century are lacking; but reports of
plays given in pantomime have preserved descriptions of elaborate settings showing that
scenery has become a very important element in
arousing interest in the drama. The first record of the Passion Play is in the form of pantomime at the celebrations which Philippe le
Bel gave in 1313. It is possible that the *Passion* was not given in its spoken form until
after it had appeared as a series of tableaux;
but it is not to be inferred that the only theatrical representations of this period were without
words. Spoken drama had developed too far
to fall into disuse for a period of a hundred
years; and the very presence of pantomimes,
both comic and serious, is evidence of the growing popularity of the drama. Undoubtedly,
miracle plays, such as those already described,

44

and comedies were being produced by actors who spoke their lines. The liturgical drama also continued to be sung at appropriate seasons. The existence of the *Miracle de Théophile* in the thirteenth century and the *Miracles de Notre Dame* in the latter half of the fourteenth century, plays so similar in form and spirit, is evidence enough that such dramas were being produced throughout the earlier half of the fourteenth century.

Godefroy de Paris in his *Chronique métrique* gives a detailed description of the scenes prepared by Philippe le Bel in 1313. There were both comic and religious tableaux, for as he says:

> Là vit-on Dieu sa mère rire;
> Renard, fisicien et mire (1. 5329–5330).[1]

Notre Dame is represented with the Three Kings of *Couloigne,* as they are curiously designated. There are ninety angels in Paradise. Thus the scene must have been large; while the chronicler claims that there were more than a hundred devils in a black and evil-smelling Hell where souls were seen tormented. The

[1] Edition Buchon.

interior of Hell was therefore visible and was
not merely called up before the mind's eye by
an entrance in the shape of a dragon's head.
On Wednesday, the account continues, a wind
blew down the curtains but everything was soon
re-arranged.   Then:

> Nostre Seignor au jugement
> I fu, et le suscitement.
> Là fu le tornai des enfans.

Christ and the apostles saying their pater-
nosters, the massacre of the innocents, the
martyrdom of St. John, Herod and Caiaphas,
Et renard chanter une espitre, were also seen.
The chronicle implies that the comic and religious scenes were juxtaposed, but this may
be a mere carelessness in style.   The author
continues:

> Crois et flos, et Hersent qui file;
> Et d'aultre part Adam et Eve;
> Et Pilate, qui ses mains lève;
> Rois à feve, et hommes sauvages
> Qui menoïent grands rigolages.

This was done by the weavers while the *coir-
roiers* represented

La vie de Renart sans faille,
Qui menjoit et poucins et paille;
Mestre Renart i fu évesque
Véu, et pape, et arcevesque;
Renart i fu en toute guise,
Si com sa vie le devise:
En bière, en crois et en cencier,
Et en maintes guises dancier.
En blanches chemises ribaus
I vit-on, lies et gais et baus.
Les rousigniax, les papegais
Ouist-on chanter de cuers gais.
Es hales estoit le bois clos,
Où maint conin estoit enclos;
C'estoit privée sauvagine,
A cui l'en batoit bien l'eschine.
Panunciaus, gonfanons, banières,
Estrumens de maintes manières
Vit-on là, et chastiax et tours;
Dames caroler de biax tours.
. . . .
Il fut trois jours en la semaine,
Serainnes, cyves et lyons,
Liépars, et maintes fictions,
Que borjois firent, por estrainne,
Par Paris toute la semaine.
Là furent borgoises parées,
Balans et dansans regardées.

Thus almost every kind of a spectacle was
offered during these days, and we see the comic

and religious scenes holding their places side
by side. The Passion Play, thus represented
in the open air, would differ little from the
spoken Passions of the fifteenth century such as
that given at Angers. Both productions would
have a large stage; and undoubtedly the scenery
of the pantomime influenced the drama in dialogue, which was produced in the open air, in regard both to the size and the setting of the stage.
There is no evidence of different levels used in
this setting, although both Heaven and Hell
were represented. The scenes were evidently
set separately, and therefore the scheme of elevation would not be carried out. The same
conditions seem to have existed later in street
mysteries,[2] and the stage of the *Résurrection* of
the thirteenth century has already been mentioned as probably being on one elevation.
Such a procedure may well have sprung from
the fact that with scenes in Heaven and Hell
set separately, say with a street intervening
or at the opposite end of a market place as at
Angers, the effect of different elevations would
be lost.

Similar settings were shown in 1389 at the

[2] See p. 118, *Mystère de la Passion* given at Rouen.

entrance of Isabeau de Bavière into Paris. At
the first gate of Saint-Denis there was *ung ciel
tout estellé, et dedens ce ciel jeunes enffans ap-
pareilliés et mis en ordonnance d'angles* . . .
*et estoit le ciel armoié très-richement des armes
de France et de Bavière.* . . . There was also
an historical scene on another scaffolding where
*estoit ordonné le Pas-Salhadin, et tous fais de
personnages, les chrestiens d'une part, et les
Sarrazins d'aultre part.* At the second gate
of Saint-Denis there was a second *ciel nué et
estellé très richement,* and within sat the
Trinity and choir boys singing as angels. As
the queen passed in her litter, Paradise
opened and two angels came from above and
placed a crown on her head. This, then, is an
attempt at realism by placing Heaven, not above
the level of the stage, for it is a separate scene,
but at least above the street where the proces-
sion passed, in order to heighten the effect of
the action. The lords and ladies next found
a scaffolding *couvert de draps de haultes lices et
encourtiné en manière d'une chambre* within
which men were playing an organ.

  The most elaborate scene was set at the gate
of the Châtelet, where there was *ung chastel*

4

*ouvré et charpenté de bois et de garites . . . et
là avoit à chascun des crestiaulx ung homme
d'armes armé de toutes pièces, et sur ce chastel
ung lit paré, ordonné et encourtiné aussi richement de toutes choses . . . et estoit ce lit ap-
pellé le lit de Justice; et là en ce lit par figure et
par personnage se gésoit Madame sainte Anne.*
The bed was guarded by twelve maidens with
naked swords. Also there was a forest scene,
for the account continues: *Ou plain de ce
chastel qui estoit contenant grant espace avoit
une garenne et grant foison de ramée.*[3] Within
this scene there were rabbits and birds and a
white deer. A lion and eagle were supposed to
issue from the woods.

These pantomimes show that scenery was
enjoyed for itself alone even during the fourteenth century, and they are indicative of the
relative grandeur of the settings which came in
the following centuries. Such scenes were also
produced in the contemporary *Miracles de
Notre Dame* and the *Passion* of the *Ste. Geneviève* collection; but undoubtedly the settings
were greatly reduced in size and beauty, for
the *Puy de Notre Dame* or the *Confrérie de la*

[3] The account is taken from Froissart.

Passion would have neither the space in an inclosed theater nor the money necessary to duplicate such scenery.

The Provençal *Martyre de Sainte Agnes*,[4] which has been dated between the last years of the thirteenth century and the first years of the fourteenth, shows a setting which combines both scenery and chairs. Heaven is represented, for the soul of Saint Agnes is brought before God; but there is nothing in the directions or the lines to indicate the position or decoration of the scene. The interior of Hell is shown, for the devils take the soul of the Saint and boil it in a cauldron in Hell. This action of course was visible. Neither Heaven nor Hell is described as carefully as the *lupanar;* and these two scenes were perhaps rather unimportant, as far as setting is concerned. The *lupanar,* however, could be entered, and the bed of Saint Agnes was shown within. This scene was evidently no improvised, summary setting which left much to the imagination. The Prefect, on the other hand, is seated *in cathedra sua,* as was the custom. The direction *Modo*

---

[4] See Annales de la Société des Lettres, Sciences, et Arts des Alpes-maritimes, vol. IV, 1877, Nice.

recedunt omnes Romani in castellum suum is
quite definite and there is little reason for
doubting that this scene and the *castellum* of
Sempronius were set. The number of scenes
was small; but this play proves that such places
as the *lupanar* were set at the beginning of the
fourteenth century. Thus one has little hesitation in believing that such scenes were also
decorated later in the century in plays like the
Miracles de Notre Dame, although practically
all of the stage directions are lost to us.

Even from these meagre data it is seen that
the art of stage decoration was developing in
the fourteenth century. The pantomimes and
tableaux which took place at the entrances of
kings and queens, undoubtedly influenced the
open air mysteries and made their stage larger
and more beautiful. In reality, an open air
mystery must have been mere pantomime to the
majority of spectators. The germ of such a
spectacle, on so vast a scale, lies in just such
scenes as those described above. In regard to
the closed theatre, the record of which probably
begins with the *Miracles de Notre Dame,* the
influence of the pantomimes would naturally be
lessened, just in proportion to the difference

existing between the two forms of drama and their stages. A strict line of demarcation must be drawn between the open air stage, which increased to great dimensions and finally fell into disuse, and the inclosed stage, whose history can be traced to the present day.

CHAPTER IV

Miracles de Notre Dame. Their Treatment of the Hell Scene. Their Stage of Two Levels. Setting of Heaven not Important. Scenes on Earth. Number of Scenes.

THE *Miracles de Notre Dame* belong to the fourteenth century. They are very important in the history of the French stage. Emile Roy, indeed, believes that "in all probability the seat of the Puy Notre Dame, the hall where it gave its representations, was in the neighborhood of the *Halles,* that is to say, not far from that *Hôpital de la Trinité* where another celebrated *confrérie* was to play the *Passion* later."[1] Starting at this point, therefore, it is possible to follow the practically uninterrupted development of the theater in Paris. While theatrical activities were by no means confined to Paris, yet the stage under a roof in the city that finally became the center of art, is of more importance

[1] Roy, Etudes sur le théâtre français du XIVe au XVIe siècles, Paris, 1902, ch. 6. The date of the founding of this Puy is given by Roy as about 1391.

than the great open air shows on temporary
stages in the provinces. This hall in which the
Miracles de Notre Dame were given is a pre-
cursor of the *Hôtel de Bourgogne,* which brings
us down to comparatively modern times.

What, then, was the stage setting of the
Miracles de Notre Dame?   Unfortunately there
are few stage directions; and with the exception of Roy, who has discussed some points of
the *mise-en-scène* though not the entire setting,
writers on the subject have given up the task
of reconstructing the scenery of these plays.
The problem is not easy to solve; but when
stage directions are lacking, the lines themselves must be made to furnish the needed
evidence.   This is a dangerous proceeding, but
since it is the only means at present of throwing
light upon the scenes of these plays, the method
must be employed for want of a better one.

Petit de Julleville has said that perhaps
there was little or no scenery; thus all mention
of rooms, palaces, etc., would be rhetorical.
But this does not seem possible, for the Middle
Ages in France bear witness to a strangely
careful and complicated stage setting wherever
stage directions are found.   The lack of direc-

tions for scenery in these plays may well have
been an omission from the manuscript rather
than an indication of the absence of scenery—
a lack which would have been remarkable. It
could hardly be possible that, in such an age of
realistic setting, forty plays, so full of action
and so dependent on scenery, should have been
produced with little or no stage decoration.
There is also one rubric in the thirty-first
Miracle (line 614) which says, referring evidently to a palace: *Ycy va le roi en sale.* This
could not mean that the king enters on the stage
or in the hall where the play was being given,
since the direction occurs in the middle of the
king's speech. Thus the word *sale* means a
piece of scenery representing a palace. In the
thirty-sixth Miracle is found the direction: *Ici
fait un po de pose et vient a sa maison.* There
can be no doubt about the word *maison.* It is
the common word for scenery. Thus the many
references to scenes of different kinds could not
all have been rhetorical. It is not possible to
believe that when windows and doors which
open and close were mentioned, there was nothing but the empty air to which the actors
pointed. It must be taken into consideration

that one company of actors was giving these
plays and the same piece of scenery could be
used again and again.   Thus an examination of
passages in different plays in which references
are made to a church or a prison will serve to
give material for reconstructing this or that
scene.

The setting representing Hell has always
been considered an important characteristic of
the stage of the Middle Ages; but it seems to
have been unimportant in the *Miracles de Notre
Dame*.   In Miracle number one the devils appear, but not a word about Hell is spoken.
Even when they leave, the lines read:

> 570.   .   .   .   .   Alons   mant,
> Car   nous   avons   ailleurs   a   faire.
>
> .   .   .   .
>
> 1386.   Alons   men   sanz   faire   demour.

Since Hell is not needed, there is no reason for
believing that it was represented either in this
play or in the one which follows it in the manuscript, for not even the devils appear in the
second Miracle.

When the devils enter in the next Miracle the
lines (882 ff.) show plainly that they are sup-

posed to meet on neutral ground before the
archdeacon. When they have the soul for
which they have come, they say that they will
carry it into Hell:

> 1031.   Or l'i menons donques bonne erre,
>   Et puis si venrons son corps querre
>   Qui la se gist.

As soon as their intention is avowed, there
is no line which shows them carrying it out.
Instead, there is a short scene between mortals
which immediately follows this speech. Then
the devil says:

> 1070.   Sathan, puis qu'en nostre meurjoye
>   Celle meschant ame avons mis.

Thus the action is related, or is "messengered,"
as is said of classic tragedy. Where one would
expect lines showing the action, were it visible,
a scene is interpolated evidently in order to
bridge the gap while the devils carry the soul
off the stage. One only needs to read these
Miracles to see how significant is the absence
of lines describing an action, for in all such
plays the lines are a running commentary on
the action, which would soon become unintel-

ligible were this not the case. When the devils
come back for the body, they load it into a
wheelbarrow and say:

1084.   Alons ment, grant bruit demenant,
            Par ceste voie.

But the body is saved even before they reach the
Hell "behind the scenes," for it was probably
not visible.

The devil appears in the sixth Miracle to St.
Jehan Crisothomes when he is praying. This
scene being finished the devil leaves, saying
(line 720): *Car se je maintenant m'en vois.*
No mention of Hell is made. These oft-recur-
ring lines point to a real exit—a rare proceeding in medieval drama, though perhaps made
necessary in this case on account of limited
stage area. The devil enters later and says
that the saint will be taken to Hell, but he
simply throws a letter into the hall of the
king and passes on. That is the extent of his
rôle. Surely no scene of Hell was represented.
The rôle of the devils in the ninth Miracle is
even shorter. They appear in the desert and
beat St. William. Then they leave, as line
1177, *Vien t'en,* shows us. Hell is not mentioned or needed.

The devil has only two speeches, in the
twelfth Miracle, of about thirty lines in all.
There is no possibility of Hell being represented. The devil merely regrets that his prey
is escaping him.

In the thirteenth Miracle the devil says:

> 348.   Alons nous en sanz demourée
>   En enfer. . . . . . .

But there is no line which even intimates that
the spectators were supposed to see the devils
reach Hell. Their scene simply finishes with
these lines, which seem to mark an exit. They
return to take the emperor to their abode, as
their final line 686, *L'en entrainnons,* plainly
says. But that is all. We do not see him put
into Hell. Again the line serves for a real or
an assumed exit. No line suggests special
scenery.

The fourteenth Miracle is entitled *"un
miracle de Nostre Dame d'un prevost que a la
requeste de saint Prist Nostre Dame delivra de
purgatoire."* In this play Purgatory is represented, and also has some of the attributes of
Hell. The *Archediacre* and Estienne are placed
there, and since they carry on a conversation

while in it, the interior must have been seen.
Such a line as *Et ce feu trop ardent et chaut*
(line 481) and others are evidence of the representation of flames. Thus it might well be a
scene in Hell itself, although it is called
Purgatory.

The devils appear in the sixteenth Miracle;
but it would be vain to attempt to prove that
Hell was represented, since it has nothing to
do with the story. The devils merely play the
usual rôle of tempters; and when they leave,
nothing is said of their returning to Hell. The
devil's last word when he leaves the pope is
(line 1235) : *Dolent m'en vois.* The scene then
continues before the pope.

In number twenty-five the devils appear in
order to carry off the souls of the emperor and
the jailor. The following lines are significant:

> 1338.   Ensemble les fera bon mettre;
>   Aussi sont il d'une convine.
>   Avant! avec moi t'achemine
>   Ysnellment.

This is the devils' final word. The play closes
after three short speeches. The above-cited
lines point to a real or assumed taking of the

souls off the stage. They almost preclude even the possibility of a Hell being shown, for when a Hell was represented torture scenes were common, and much, instead of little, was made of such an opportunity. But in this case one can almost see the devils carrying their burden away. If they did not do this, but placed the souls in Hell and tormented them, why do these lines occur and these alone?

Miracle number thirty-six shows the devils at the bed-side of the sick merchant and later arguing their case before God. Instead of going back to Hell when they leave, we know from lines 594 ff. that they are supposed to go to the *rue du Plastre,* which must have been behind the scenes, since the scene which is suggested does not take place before the eyes of the spectators. Thus it would be impossible to conceive a Hell shown in this play.

Out of the forty plays of this collection there are thirty in which devils do not appear and therefore there is no possibility of a scene in Hell. Of the ten remaining plays in which such a scene might have been expected, in nine Hell was either behind the scenes or not required at all. The conclusion is that the *Mira-*

cles de Notre Dame were plays in which Hell
was of no importance in regard to the setting.
This is evidence in favor of the theory we are
trying to establish, that in this period of the
development of the stage decoration, Hell was
not represented as a general rule. In these
productions, with one exception, there is no
smoke escaping, no infernal din within a yawn-
ing dragon's mouth, although the lines show
once that the devils make an uproar on the
stage (No. 3, lines 1084 ff.). The setting of
Hell and the use of devils seem to have lost in
importance since the *Adam* play. The devils
are not seen running about and cutting up ca-
pers among the spectators; they are only introduced when their presence is necessary to
the story. They play their legitimate part and
then, if we can believe the lines, they leave the
stage. Their rôles are generally short and often
insignificant in comparison to the others. The
word *enfer* occurs very rarely. The gates are
only mentioned once, and this is but a passing
reference which does not imply scenery. Finally, up to this point, there is no evidence of
the far-famed and somewhat overworked dragon's head. It is also significant that even though

devils are in these plays, Hell does not usually
appear. It hardly seems possible, therefore,
that the producers of these plays were accustomed to seeing mysteries in which there was
a realistic representation of Hell with its dragon's head, smoke, and frightful din.

The fourteenth Miracle, in which Purgatory
is represented, is the one exception; for the
scene, though called Purgatory, resembles Hell
in the fact that the souls were burned. Yet
even if it be granted that a scene resembling
the setting of Hell appeared on this stage of
one out of forty plays, none of the conclusions
is in any way shaken. As is seen by the above-
cited title of the Miracle, a scene in Purgatory
is demanded. The play could hardly exist
without this scene. Therefore when such settings were necessary they could be constructed.
It was not because of any difficulty in mounting
such scenes that they were generally lacking.
The reason would seem to be that the importance of such scenery in arousing interest had
not yet impressed itself on the producers of
these plays. The *Miracles de Notre Dame*—
plays of the fourteenth century—are evidence
in favor of the theory that Hell played an un-

important part in the medieval stage up to the
fifteenth century, and that its careful setting
and especially the setting of the entrance in the
shape of a dragon's head, belong to a much
later period than has been believed heretofore.

For all but one of these plays the stage must
have consisted of two levels: Heaven and Earth.
It is true that in this play line 593 reads: *Q'en
purgatoire est descenduz.* It is a question
whether the realism went so far as to place the
scene of Purgatory on a lower level in the setting corresponding to the evident idea of the
author. The following lines also refer to the
conception of Purgatory.

> 910.   Las! Qui est ce qui de ce val
>   Meschant, chetif, lait et hideux,
>   Puant, orrible et tenebreux
>   Me veult oster?

No doubt the place was dark and partook of the
nature indicated by some of these adjectives;
and it may well have been on a lower level than
the rest of the scenes, for the realism of the
medieval setting is always remarkable. In any
case it must be borne in mind that this scene
is an exception as far as these plays are con-

5

cerned; and the general rule was a stage of two levels.

The decoration of Heaven was evidently not elaborate. It plays a comparatively unimportant part in the setting. The scene was surely placed above the stage proper. Evidence of this is found in such lines spoken in Heaven as: *en une chappelle* || *La dessoubz* (No. 17, line 1130–1). *Descendez a terre* (No. 36, line 963). On the other hand there are the corresponding lines spoken on Earth: *Ralons nous ent, mesnie doulce* || *Es cieulx la sus* (No. 6, lines 1383–4).[2] This arrangement also makes its appearance about this time in the *Miracles de Ste. Geneviève.*[3] The two levels were undoubtedly connected by stairs, since the angels pass up and down.

God was seated on a throne in Heaven, as is shown by the line *Car il est ou hault trone assis* (No. 3, line 800), and by *Dieu, qui est lassus ou throsne* (Miracle No. 35, line 157). As for the angels, many speeches of Notre Dame begin "*sus*"; but this word may

---

[2] Such references may be easily found in almost any of these plays.

[3] See p. 85ff.

mean "up" only in the sense of "let us go."
However, the line *Mes amis, levez sus, levez*
(No. 13, line 1500) spoken to the angels
would show that they also were sitting. As
soon as Notre Dame is on Earth in the fourteenth Miracle she is seated, as she says, *en
ceste chaiére* (line 840). This is a common
action and was probably done to show respect
and lend dignity to the character. We not only
find a chair placed for Notre Dame or God
when either comes to Earth, noted in the lines,
but also in Miracle No. 36 we find the action
implied by the lines is proved by a stage direction. Line 348 reads: *Alez m'un siége la jus
mettre.* Then the stage direction follows: *Ici
viennent chantant, et quant Diex est assis et
Notre Dame, le tiers ange va au malade et dit.*
Thus taking into consideration that the oft-re-
curring "*sus*" is sometimes made entirely clear
by the word "*levez*," also that a chair was
placed on Earth for divine characters, and that
it was the custom to have God and the angels
seated in later plays, finally that we have direct
references to the *hault throsne* of God, it may be
concluded that in these miracles God sat upon
a throne surrounded by his angels, who were

also seated, in a Heaven raised on a level above that of Earth.

This is all the information which can be gained of the position and setting of Heaven; but the very fact that the lines give so few details is evidence that Heaven, as well as Hell, was relatively unimportant in the setting of these plays and did not dominate the scene as it did in the great mysteries of a later date. The scenes in Heaven are very short and without much importance as far as the action is concerned. They consist of only a few lines in which God or Notre Dame bids one or the other to descend with the angels to Earth. It is on Earth that the occupants of Heaven play their real parts and speak the most of their lines. Therefore it is natural that the scenery for Heaven should be unimportant in these semi-profane plays, for these Miracles are a long step from the religious drama in which the setting of Heaven attracted such attention. The Miracles hold a middle ground between the religious and the profane drama, in regard to both subject matter and stage decoration. The scene of the profane drama was on one level. The scene of the religious drama was at least on two and perhaps on three levels.   It showed the beauties of Heaven and the horrors of Hell. In these plays Heaven is only an episode in the production, while Hell is hardly represented at all.   The appearance and effect of such a stage inclosed in a hall must have been very different from the stage of the open air mystery.   But this stage is none the less important as a type, although it may be less of a curiosity to the modern mind than the great spectacles which were to come; for take away the Heaven of the *Miracles de Notre Dame* and the stage will resemble very closely the setting which Hardy found and accepted and which existed in the sixteenth century.

The scenes on Earth, where the real drama was acted, were quite carefully set.   As has been said, the different scenes in these plays could be used again and again; and comparison of the several references to a common scene will serve to reconstruct it with comparative exactness.

The scene of the church occurs in twenty of the plays, and it must have been carefully set. The interior was visible, since in the fortieth Miracle we find the line 1730, *Qu'en ceste eglise*

ci l'amaines. Also line 1813, *Lez cest autel,*
shows there was an altar within the church.
This altar sometimes represents merely a shrine.
In many plays a sermon is given, and in these
miracles a reference to a pulpit or *eschaffaut*
is found upon which the preacher stood and
gave the sermon. Thus in No. 13, lines 384–5:

> Car nostre evesque en l'eschafaut
> Voy ja monté qui le fera.

The sermon is listened to by the characters in
the play. In the twelfth Miracle line 31 says:
Voulentiers a l'église iray. This is followed
out; and then, as lines 50–55 inform us, they
all sit down and listen to the sermon. Therefore in addition to the altar there were places
to sit down—there are references to this fact
throughout the plays—and also a pulpit. There
was scenery for a chapel distinct from that of
the church, since in the seventeenth Miracle
both the church and the chapel are needed, and
in the thirty-third Miracle the hermit mentions
his chapel, saying (line 1228): *En ma chappelle
m'en iray.* In the sixteenth Miracle a chapel
is built on the stage; and when it is finished
the following lines show it completed:

1581.   Fondée est ferme conme tour
         Ici endroit ceste chappelle.

Scenery for a hermitage is demanded in
eleven Miracles, and the thirty-third play gives
evidence that it must have been well worked
out, since line 1215, *Vueil donc qu'en ce lit
vous couchiez,* shows an interior and a bed.
The tenth Miracle says of the hermit's cell
(lines 148–9):

> Avis m'est que le voy seoir,
> Le chief hors de sa fenestrelle.

It does not seem to be going too far in the way
of conjecture to suppose a window from the
direct reference to one in the lines.   It must
always be kept in mind that the stage setting
of the Middle Ages was exact from the point of
view that the stage directors tried to represent
everything, and everything at once.   One is far
from claiming modern exactness for the setting
of these plays; but judging from the care with
which scenes were set which are clearly described by the stage directions, one does not
hesitate to reconstruct the small hermitage with
its interior visible, with a bed, when necessary,
and a window.   There is a miniature in the

manuscript which shows just such a cell, and the interior is made visible by removing the wall which would face the audience. The possibility of the hermitage itself not existing and of references to it being rhetorical is entirely precluded by an action which takes place in the thirtieth Miracle. The hermitage is pointed out with a light in it; and afterward it is burnt to the ground during the action of this play.

The hermitage is generally found in a forest; and a forest scene is called for by the lines in ten of the plays, while in the thirty-seventh Miracle it is spoken of as an orchard. People are lost in the forest and there are far too many direct references to the scene to permit of the belief that it was not represented, especially in the *Miracle de Berthe,* where a great part of the action passes in a forest. As for the word *deserte,* it is used for the forest itself in this Miracle; but there are also references to a *deserte* in five other plays, and no doubt it was shown in some way. These two scenes would be easily improvised.

The prison was a scene which was very often used. There are constant references to entering it, and the characters speak from the interior, which was therefore visible. The twenty-fourth Miracle gives evidence of a door and window in line 376: *Sa, sa! boutez vous par cest huis*, and line 469: *Egar! vezla une fenestre.* Line 273 of the thirty-second Miracle brings us to the conclusion that this door was no mere opening, for it can be locked: *Cest huis a la clef fermeray.* The lines which refer to doors, windows, and interiors are here given so much importance because, up to the present time, no one has attempted to show just how much scenery was used to represent these different places. To judge from miniatures, although these must not be entirely trusted, a palace generally consisted merely of a canopy and a throne. Therefore the question arises as to how a prison was shown. Were there walls and doors for such a scene? These plays give evidence that such scenes were carefully set because the action needs such exactness.

The piece of scenery representing an inn was frequently set. In the eighteenth Miracle Theodore says of the inn: *Leens me fauldra hosteller* (line 656). Supper is served on a table: *Nous avons assez longuement Sis a table*

(line 740). If the action be followed, which is
indicated by the lines, there must have been
more than one room for the inn.   The *fille* and
the *valet* are in a separate room, and Theodore
who is also at the inn summons the *valet* " *de
ceens* " (line 844).   The *valet* then says to the
*fille: Cy ne puis, m'amie, estre plus. Je vois
la, sire* (line 846).   This, as well as the preceding lines, is evidence that the interior of this
second room was visible.   There is also a third
room for Theodore implied in the action, but it
is not strictly necessary.   It will be shown later
that in some of the palaces more than one room
is absolutely requisite.   It is therefore not surprising that an inn with more than one room
is found.   In fact the possibility of an inn
separated into three rooms must not be considered as remote.   In view of the system of
multiple stage decoration it is extremely probable, for an inn of three rooms would be as
easily arranged as three separated pieces of
scenery.

There is scenery required for an abbey in
six of the Miracles.   In the eighteenth a cell
in the abbey is also shown apart from the rest
of the scene.   Theodore's cell is pointed out to

him by the abbot: *Si sera la en celle cele* (line
1391).   Also Theodore takes the *fils* to his cell
and he dies there.   This is another case in which
there must have been two compartments for the
same scene.   In the fortieth Miracle an altar is
shown in the abbey (line 1121).

In the plays of this collection which demand
a more complicated setting a ship and a sea are
needed.   The ship occurs in Nos. 27, 29, 30,
and 34.   It surely appeared on the stage or else
the following lines would be meaningless in the
twenty-seventh miracle:

> 1078.   A celle roche la menrons
>   Qui est assez avant en mer.
>   .   .   .   .
> 1090.   Baudoin, vessel prest avez:
>   Regardez.   Touz quatre ens entrons
>   Et d'y aler nous delivrons.
>   Entrez ens, dame.

They arrive at the rock in the sea.   Thus the
whole action, to be intelligible and not to be
mere meaningless pantomime, must have been
accompanied by scenery.

Other scenes which are demanded are a stable,
for the *Miracle de la Nativité;* a stronghold,
occurring in two plays; a tower, which can be

opened and closed; springs, wells, and ditches, all of which it was quite possible and necessary to represent. As for the scenery of cities corresponding to such lines as those which tell us the characters have arrived in Rome or Jerusalem, it is difficult to decide whether any special scenery marked such places or not. If we follow the evidence of miniatures, we must conclude that a gate, perhaps marked with the name of the city, was shown. But it seems unnecessary to have such a device to show, for instance, that such and such a palace is in Rome. It is more probable that such lines were merely for the information of the audience. Thus it is to be believed that cities were not formally represented, but that any *maison* or group of *maisons* naturally stood for any city where it was supposed to be. Even in the case of such scenes as the market place in Jerusalem the scene may well have been on neutral ground, for it must be remembered that neutral ground was necessary and very useful in the scheme of stage decoration. Roads and ways ought to be considered as neutral ground. Characters met and talked on it, and battles were fought there. Such places as the road to

Jerusalem or to Egypt have been too often[4] considered as distinct scenes and counted into the number of places to be represented. In reality they were definite places to the spectators, but seem to have been unmarked by special scenery.

Another point in which exception must be taken to Petit de Julleville when one reckons the number of scenes of any play is in not necessarily assigning a *maison* to a character who is simply summoned. For, as far as the action is concerned, if not in reality, this character leaves the stage after the scene with the person to whom he has been summoned. There is no reason why such a character should have a *maison* provided; such a scene is not necessary to the action and any reference made to it seems to be rhetorical. Also, only in very few cases are such references found. Generally the words *je le voy la* occur, which being wholly indefinite must mean neutral ground. They merely point the person out to the audience. However, even if there was scenery for these characters, only one or two plays would be affected, and only one or two unimportant

[4] See Petit de Julleville, Les Mysteres, vol. 1, p. 105.

maisons would be added.   Thus the results of
the investigations as a whole would not be
affected.

As to the *ostels,* palaces, and other *maisons*
which were represented, they must have been
as complete as the other scenes.   In three of the
later Miracles, Nos. 33, 34 and 39, we find a
throne mentioned.   *Voy la en son throsne seoir*
(No. 33, line 1045) refers to the palace of the
pope.   In the thirty-ninth Miracle, Clothilde is
seated on a throne and the *arcevesque* addresses
her as follows:

> 2230.   De moy en si hault siége embatre,
> Dame, ne me requerez pas;
> De me seoir ici em bas
> Me doit souffire.

As has already been shown, the chair or throne
was a common setting from the time of the
earliest liturgical plays.   In this collection of
plays there are frequent references to sitting
down in these thrones.   Therefore every *maison*
in which there was a person of some rank probably contained a throne on which he was seated
in state.   The king was surrounded by his retainers.   The pope had guards, who stood at

the gate of his palace, as is shown in Miracle No. 16: *Ly lairay je passer la porte* (line 1098). Doors are mentioned frequently. The lines *Je voi de cy la porte* || *Ouverte du manoir le roi* (No. 29, lines 260–1) might be considered as rhetorical if we had not already found references to doors in other scenes, such as that of the prison, which could not be rhetorical. In the thirty-ninth Miracle evidence of a door in Clothilde's house is furnished by the line: *Ce sac derrier cest huis ici* (line 328). There are rooms which require a bed as a setting; and a room hung with draperies is necessary to the action in the thirty-first Miracle, in which occurs the line *D'arriére ces courtines dame* (line 347). Some of the houses must have been divided into more than one room, as was the case with the inn. As a rule, however, only one room was needed. A table is often set for a meal, and the proof of this is found in one of the very few stage directions which are contained in these plays: *Cy met on la table devant l'emperiére pour mengier* (Miracle No. 25).

There is great divergence in the number of *maisons* or real scenes needed for each play,

but in no case does the amount of scenery required become manifestly impossible for a stage
in a hall.   It is possible to estimate the number
of scenes constructed for each play, although
there may be a difference of opinion as to
whether a certain *maison,* implied but not mentioned by the lines, was shown or not.   Yet this
would not materially change the conclusions.
It would simply mean that one or two plays
would need one scene more or less.   For instance, in the ninth Miracle there is no line
referring directly to the house of the pope; but
since he is found seated on a throne in other
plays, we can safely assume that he was found
thus in this play.   The same is true of scenes
before a king.   In the fifteenth Miracle the mid-
wife is summoned from *son hostel.*   This may
or may not be rhetorical.   It is not a scene
which is needed.   Also no scenery is indicated
for a scene before a judge in this play, and
probably none was shown;[5] but since in counting these scenes as represented we only have
six scenes in all, the question as to how many
scenes were shown in this play is of little consequence.   It is in comparatively few plays

[5] Cf. setting for *Pathelin,* p. 218.

that this question arises, and only those whose lines furnish full information in regard to the scenery will be used as examples of the stage of these plays.

It is to be taken for granted that Heaven was always represented above the rest of the scenery in all these Miracles. The tenth Miracle is an example of a simple setting which consisted of a hermit's cell, a chapel, and a house. In the eleventh Miracle there is a hermit's cell, a wood, and a merchant's house. The fourteenth needs an altar, the house of the archdeacon, Purgatory, the pope's house, and a chair for *Notre Dame* when she visits Earth. The setting of the sixteenth Miracle is a church, the house of the *penancier,* the house of the pope, the house of the pope's mother, a chapel constructed during the play, and the house of the curé. The thirty-first Miracle needs two palaces, in one of which there are two rooms separated by curtains, a forest, a chapel and the house of Simon. The thirty-second presents a more complicated setting: a palace of two rooms, a forest, a prison, an inn, a house for the *charbonnier,* a temple or church, a boat on the sea, and the house of the *tabellion.* The thirty-third is also complicated and demands the house of Robert, the peasant's house, an abbey, a forest, the house of the duke (probably divided into two rooms), a hermitage with a chapel, the emperor's stronghold, and the pope's house. The thirty-seventh Miracle shows a church, a palace with a throne and a separate room, the temple in Jerusalem with an altar, a forest, a boat, an inn, Isabel's house, a prison, and the emperor's palace with two rooms. The setting of the thirty-ninth Miracle consists of two palaces (one of which has two rooms), a church, a fountain, Clothilde's house, and Gondebaut's house. The fortieth demands the house of Euphemion, the palace of Honorius, a room for Sabine, an abbey, a church, a boat, and the pope's house. In the latter Miracles there may have been one *maison* more or less needed by the whole play. A typical stage of these plays would show six or seven scenes, which is the number used by most of Hardy's plays. Such a stage could be easily set in a hall. The plays which needed eleven or twelve scenes would cause no trouble if mounted out of doors, but it is supposed that all of the *Miracles de Notre Dame* were given in an inclosed hall. If this is true, either the stage must have been larger than that of the *Hôpital de la Trinité* or of the *Hôtel de Bourgogne,* which were quite spacious;[6] or scenery may have been changed or renewed during the performance. At any rate an indoor stage in Paris with twelve scenes set simultaneously is uncommon during the period in which we know that inclosed theaters existed. After 1402 the size of the stage of the *Hôpital de la Trinité* makes that number of scenes impossible; and this stage remained for over a century and a quarter. The rather large number of scenes required by some of these Miracles foreshadows the great out-door spectacles of the fifteenth century; but if any of these longer Miracles were given later in the *Hôpital de la Trinité* or in a hall of like dimensions, either a part of the action was left out or scenery was changed.

When given by the *Puy de Notre Dame,* however, a large enough stage was probably provided. What scenes were needed must have been set with care and exactness. Yet scenery has not yet reached that period in its development when it is used as a delight to the eye.

[6] See p. 192.

It is an aid to the understanding of the action;
but except in the number of scenes there are
few signs of the elaborateness which character-
izes the later mysteries.　Once a character
says: *Je voi merveilleuse clarté Descendre des
cieulx la amont* (Miracle No. 13, lines 581–2),
but such lines are rare.　The productions of
this Puy were not great spectacles.　They
began with simple plays accompanied by simple
setting.　There is a development, a step for-
ward in complexity; but the *Miracles de Notre
Dame* mark a period of transition toward the
great spectacular plays, while they also show a
type of a simple stage decoration of few scenes
which will continue to exist in the indoor
theatres throughout the Middle Ages and the
Renaissance.[7]

[7] *Miracles de Notre Dame*, Paris et Robert.　Paris,
1876.　(Soc. des anc. texts frçs.)

CHAPTER V

THE *Miracles* contained in the Jubinal publication of the manuscript of *Ste. Geneviève* have also been made the subject of investigations carried on by Roy. Since the répertoire of this collection corresponds to that of the *Confrérie de la Passion* as stated in their famous *lettres patentes* of 1402, he believes that these plays are the ones mentioned when this body is authorized to *faire et jouer quelque Mistere que ce soit, soit de la dicte Passion et Resurrection ou autre quelconque tant de saincts comme de sainctes que ilz vouldront elire et mettre sus.* The date of these representations is therefore placed at the latter part of the fourteenth and the beginning of the fifteenth century. It is very important to know their setting, for the *Confrérie de la Passion* and their dramas hold

the stage in Paris at least until 1548, when their
trouble began in earnest. These plays must be
conceived as being given regularly within doors,
instead of occupying a temporary stage set up
at the expense of a whole town. There was
nothing to hinder an open air performance, but
the real stage of these plays was probably the
Hôpital de la Trinité, whose dimensions are
given as 6 by 21½ *toises.*[1] Thus the stage in
such a hall was not large. But such a stage is
none the less typical of the Middle Ages. It
is even more important for the evolution of the
drama than the large temporary stages in the
open air. The *Miracles de Ste. Geneviève* are
well adapted to a small stage. The plays could
be given separately or collectively. The demands made upon the stage director could
hardly have been difficult to fulfill at any time.
They form a cycle from which different plays
could be selected.

These miracle plays seem to have treated the
setting of Hell as did the *Miracles de Notre
Dame,* that is, Hell was generally behind the
scenes. Devils appear in the *Martyre de St.
Pierre et de St. Pol,* but Hell itself is not rep-

[1] See p. 191. The *toise* was 1 metre, 949 mil.

resented by a formal scene. When Simon is killed, the first devil says: *Ou puis d'enfer vous porteron.* A stage direction follows which reads: *Cy l'emportent hors du champ en uslant.* The pit of Hell is thus *hors du champ,* or behind the scenes; and the spectator merely saw an exit. Later in the play Nero is killed and the devils cry out: *Ou puis d'enfer te porteron.* A stage direction then shows the following action: *Lors l'emportent et puis le jetent en une chaudière assise un pou haut enmy le champ.* They tell him that now he will know what Hell is. Then they blow under the cauldron and make some smoke; but, as the direction says, they soon cease. The second devil speaks:

> Néron, encore pis te feron.
> A Lucifer te porteron.

Then comes the stage direction: *Cy le portent hors du champ;* and again it is seen that Hell proper, where Lucifer stays, is behind the scenes. It is not correct to say that the cauldron represented a scene in Hell. It was placed before the eyes of the spectators as one of the infernal tortures and was introduced to satisfy the medieval demand for horrors.[2]

[2] Cohen holds a different view, *op. cit.,* p. 93.

The other miracle in this collection in which devils appear is the miracle of the child thrown into a well and resuscitated by Ste. Geneviève. After the devils have obtained the soul of the child, the author resorts to this means of getting them out of the spectators' eyes as far as the action is concerned. Satan says:

> . . . . .Or nous séons
> Et dedens nos papiers véons.

The stage direction carries out this action: *Lors se sieent et regardent en leurs roulez et soient jusques à tant que les anges viegnent.* This means is employed to get the devils out of the way, because evidently Hell is not represented, or they would have gone to their natural abode.   When the soul is taken from the demons after a sharp struggle, the direction says: *Cy s'en fuient.*   This must mean, off the stage; and there is nothing to show that a scene from Hell was used in these plays which deal with the conversion and martyrdom of the saints.

However, a scene in Hell is needed in one of the miracle plays which deal with Ste. Geneviève, for Raphael is directed to take *une*

ymagete soubz le couverteur et la tiegne suz son
bras senestre en ly monstrant à la destre enfer.
The soul of Ste. Geneviève is shown in Hell, of
which the tortures are described in a few lines.
The episode is short and unimportant. The
scene may have been a kind of tableau; but it
does not occur again in these Miracles. The
fact that the scene occurs but once shows that
the Hell scene was by no means indispensable.
Here were plenty of chances to use it, which
were allowed to slip by. Even though it does
not seem probable, let it be granted that, because in one of these plays a scene in Hell was
used, such a scene was also used in the others
noted above, since they all belonged to the same
confrérie; yet the setting does not gain in importance. It is merely an exit. There is no
evidence of a dragon's mouth. At best, the
setting of Hell in miracle plays must be regarded as an unimportant episode in the whole
production. It is in the mysteries that the
scenes in Hell are so carefully set; and the
mystery plays belong mostly to the fifteenth
century. The stage without a dragon's head,
even with no representation of Hell, is none
the less typical of the Middle Ages than the

stage on which the horrors of Hell occupied a large place. Indeed any attempt to reduce the stage setting to a type is likely to prove disastrous.

Considering first only the plays of this collection which deal with the saints, it is found that Heaven was placed above the stage, as is proved by the stage direction in the *Conversion de S. Pol: Lors voisent en passant par dessoulz Paradis.* The scene evidently did not extend over the whole stage, nor around three sides of it as is shown in some miniatures, for the actors are directed to walk under it, and also *Damas* is placed *en costé Paradis.* Its exact location is doubtful. In later plays, it was at one side of the stage and Hell on the other.[3] In the preceding miracle, which may be joined to this one, the lines show God seated in Heaven and Christ on his right hand. There are also angels in Heaven who, as in the *Miracles de Notre Dame,* sing rondels.

The setting of these plays was simple. There is nothing in the lines of the *Martyre de Saint Estienne* to show any scenery, except Heaven, or any change of the place of action.

[3] See p. 118.

There are chairs for the characters and evidently some of them stand on a raised platform. Lisbie is directed: *Cy descende d'en hault et voise devant St. Denis.* Another direction reads: . . . *Fescennin soit ou plus hault ciége,* while Simon mounts *un pou hault* in order to call the devils. Such an arrangement may have been employed to raise certain characters above the rest of the stage, in order that they might be seen more easily, especially if the actor were supposed to be on a throne.[4]

The question as to how cities were represented at this period rises again. *Damas,* for instance, is *en costé Paradise.* Was it merely represented by its provost and citizens? Was there any scenery to mark Athens beyond the four altars? Were Rome and Paris merely places where such and such an action took place, but undecorated by scenery beyond a throne or any *maison* supposed to be in that place? There is no reason for conjecturing that there were other special settings at this time on this stage. Whatever scenery occurs in these plays is merely an aid to the understanding of the action.

[4] See p. 193.

There is evidence of a real *maison* in the
prison, which can be entered, and whose interior and exterior were visible, as is shown by
the direction: *En la chartre soient vestemens
. . . autel et calice et du pain.* That such a
scene should have walls is made necessary by
the action. There is also a direction *en monstrant lit et table* which refers to an inn. It is
impossible to say whether this scene had a wall
or not. But there are few such scenes and it
really makes little difference, therefore, whether
in these plays they were inclosed on one or two
sides.

If thrones are granted to dignitaries,—and
there is little reason for conjecturing anything
else showing a palace—about all the scenery
and properties needed for these plays besides
the scenes just discussed are: a ditch, table and
chairs for the house of *Catulle, chevaus de fust,
greil,* and a *four.* These plays do not need
much scenery nor do they lend themselves
readily to any elaborate setting. They are too
full of scholastic discussions. Few scenes were
needed if the plays were given separately. But
they could be combined and thus it is difficult
to say just how many scenes were set at once.

The *Conversion de S. Pol* would need *Damas,*
probably represented by its citizens; a provost;
and a *maison* for the Virgin. If the *Conversion de S. Denis* were joined to it then four
altars would be added to the setting. A stage
direction speaks of a *logeis* for the philosopher
and his wife, but this does not necessarily mean
scenery. It refers to the place of the actors on
the stage rather than any set scene, for the direction *voisent en leur logeis* is given when the
stage is to be cleared in the next play, and the
scene changes to "before Nero." A throne for
Nero and a tomb are the only scenes added if
this third play be given. Finally if the *Martyre
de S. Denis* be given, the only new scenes to
be set are the prison, an inn, the house of *Catulle,* and a ditch. Thus in any case the stage
would not be overcrowded as there are few
real scenes, since the chairs of dignitaries do
not count. Also nothing would hinder scenery
being removed or used twice. Thus again one
must imagine a stage with few scenes.

The *Miracles de Ste. Geneviève* also require
very little scenery. Heaven with God and the
angels is above the stage, as is usual at this
period; and there is one vision of Hell, although

the scene does not seem to have been much used, for at least there is no evidence that the devils use it even as an exit. The plays are very short; and, if taken separately, only one or two real scenes would be set. Even if they were played together the stage would not have been overcrowded.

The house in which Ste. Geneviève was born is referred to very clearly by the lines, and the scene must have been set. The child is told not to pass the door; but she goes where *une queue soit ou pierres comme la gueule de .i. puis.* This same well probably served in the later Miracle of the child thrown into a well by the devils. This direction also serves to show how such scenes were constructed.

The home of Ste. Geneviève near Paris is described very carefully as follows: *Lors se tiegne devant Paris un pou avant ou champ, et illecques soit un petit autel suz le quel soit l'image Nostre Dame, et devant l'autel une fourmete pour soy mettre à oroison, et bien près soit son lit fait de une table en hault et un povre couverteur dessuz et. i. oreillier de bois.* When such care is taken to prescribe the setting of this scene it is probable that if there had been special scenery for Paris, it, too, would have been mentioned. Lectree is marked by an altar with the image of St. Denis upon it. The direction: *Cy retournent à leur hostel,* which refers to the sick girl and her mother and which occurs at the end of the play, hardly refers to a scene. The *hostel* is not necessary to the action unless it was the sick girl's bed, in which case it would be easily represented. There is no evidence that it was a separate *maison,* carefully set. All of the scenery necessary for the action is described by the directions. As has been seen, the places represented are few and the settings, while realistic, are not elaborate. The scene in Heaven is not the one which held the eyes of the audience; but the interest centered upon Earth. Realistic simplicity is the chief characteristic of the stage decoration.

The *Vie de S. Fiacre* is only another example of this simplicity. The stage was probably set with a boat, a church with an altar, a hermitage which can be entered and which is built on the stage, Heaven, and perhaps a *maison* for the *Pucelle.* This play, however, is interrupted by a farce in which scenery is needed for a tavern, as is shown by the lines:

> En ceste chambre cy derrière
> Vous séez; lieu y a privé.

There are lacunae in the *Nativité* of this collection; but the scenery can none the less be reconstructed with little probable error. Earthly Paradise and Heaven seem to be the same scene in this play, as far as can be judged from the lines. It has already been pointed out that in the *Adam* play Paradise, while on a higher level, could not be considered as a scene representing Heaven. It will be seen later that in the *Mistère du Vieil Testament,* the two scenes are quite distinct. Also in this play it must be remembered that the part of Paradise in which the Tree of Life stands and from which Adam and Eve are driven would present quite a different appearance from that part of Paradise occupied by God and the angels. Therefore, in reality, there were two scenes. The line spoken by God: *Qui là jus gardent les aigneaux* is evidence that Heaven was above the stage.

Hell is necessary to the action and even its interior was shown. The devil says:

> Adam, venez en noz maison
> Ou premier estage d'enfer.

That this implied action is carried out is proved by the stage direction: *Adam en enfer die.* Thus Adam and the prophets were seen in the *premier estage d'enfer,* or Limbo, as this scene will be called later. Do these words point to a scene set on a lower level? It must be borne in mind that the stage was set with remarkable realism; and the same feeling which would cause Heaven to be placed above the stage would naturally cause Hell to be set below the level of Earth. The lines in this play spoken from Hell: *Ha roy Jhésus toy demandons, Dessens tost,* are in favor of this theory. This does not necessarily mean that the stage was built in three stories; but there is evidence that more than two levels were shown on the stage. The stage directions and lines of the plays which follow the *Nativité* in this collection may also be cited, since all of these plays were probably produced on the same stage.

After the creation the scene changes and Caesar's palace is shown. There is more than a mere throne, for after the line: *Or alons là hors véoir, sire,* comes the stage direction: *Cy voisent hors de leur eschaufault et regardent le*

7

ciel. There are also some idols represented, one of them being the statue of Jupiter.

The temple was shown, for Mary asks that she may be allowed to remain *en ce temple;* but there may have been only a chair or seat to represent the house of Joseph, since, after he has been away Mary, says to him: *Venez vous delez moi séoir.* A *maison* is not necessary for the action. After Gabriel has announced to Mary that she will bear a child, a dove *fait par bonne manière* descends.

The stable must have been carefully represented. It is called a *hale désordonnée.* The child is placed in the manger, and the cattle are plainly pointed out by the lines. There is nothing to show a house for the *Maréchal,* but there is a distinct scene when Joseph asks him for fire and *le mete en son giron.* Such scenes and the scenes with the shepherds hardly demand formal scenery. The setting for this play can not be called complicated, even if these scenes be counted. Yet it is sufficient for the action. Such properties as the dove and a heavenly light which is supposed to illumine the stable are indications of the growing importance of scenery and machinery introduced for its own sake and not merely to make the action intelligible.

The *Geu des Trois Roys* which follows the
Nativité does not show much advance beyond
the liturgical drama dealing with the same subject. There is nothing to prove that the Three
Kings had *maisons*. Probably they came each
"as if from his own kingdom" as they did in
the older drama. The star was represented as
usual. The stable, however, had an added touch
of realism in the animals. This scene was
surely the one just described in the *Nativité*.
In order to represent the journey the kings are
directed as follows: *Cy voisent entour le champ.*
They arrive before Herod; and there is no
direct evidence that the palace was represented
by any scenery except a chair or throne. Yet
Caesar's palace, which was marked by a *maison*
in the preceding play, is not needed in this play.
The same setting may well have been used for
Herod's palace, which plays an important part
in this drama. In reality, this *Geu des Trois
Roys* is a second act to the *Nativité* and such
changing of scenery would naturally occur.
This *maison* would then be guarded and would
explain both the line: *Garder les pors et la
cité,* and the stage direction: *Cy facent semblant de aler garder.* . . . In fact since Hell

is used as an exit when the devils carry Herod there, it is quite possible the setting of the *Nativité* was but little changed. The temple would help to represent *la cité,* and whatever represented the house of Joseph would remain set. The Tree of Life and the idols are not needed; but otherwise the appearance of the stage is hardly altered.

The setting of the *Passion* was somewhat different. The interior of Simon's house must have been shown. There are several scenes which take place within it including that of the last supper when a table is set. The sepulchre of Lazarus is also indispensable to the action. There is one *maison,* however, which is pointed out by the lines, but which one is inclined to put behind the scenes even though that region, which is so useful to modern drama, was but little used in the drama of the Middle Ages. Christ bids two of the disciples go *ou chastel contre vous* where they will find the ass upon which he will ride into Jerusalem. Now the *chastel* itself is not needed as far as the action is concerned and the actor might well have pointed behind the scenes, even though the animal itself was on the stage. The scene is

not important. To set it would have complicated the stage unnecessarily. The stage setting
was simultaneous and complex but it was not
chaotic. The tendency to allow the imagination
to dwell upon the curiosities of the open air
spectacles is likely to make one forget the small
stage where the area was limited.

Once in Jerusalem, Christ is led before Annas,
Caiaphas, Herod, and Pilate. The palace of
Herod has been discussed above. The houses
or palaces of the other characters were undoubtedly represented by chairs, at least; and probably there was more scenery. Pilate speaks of
his *hostel*. The house of Annas is mentioned.
At any rate there are four distinct scenes. The
blacksmith's forge must have added an interesting bit of realism, for the fire is placed within it
and the nails are forged. Calvary was elevated
as is shown by the line: *Jusques en ce tertre
là devant.* The cross is naturally placed upon
this eminence. Heaven is above the stage as
usual. Evidence of this arrangement is found
in the stage direction: *Les Angles sus.* A
mercier is introduced and cloth is bought of
him. Also the three Marys go to an *épicerie*.
These scenes, while they demand certain prop-

erties, would not need special scenery representing two shops beyond the goods themselves which were displayed. The sepulchre, which played so great a part in the liturgical drama, was not lacking in this play.

Finally both the interior and exterior of Hell are visible. Jesus, on the outside, says: *Princes d'enfer, ouvrez vos portes.* Satan, within, says to the devils:

> A ces portes fort soustenir.
> Fay que cil huis soient verroulé.

It is to be noted that the word *gates* or *doors* is still used for the entrance just as it is in the *Adam* play. These gates are bolted. This fact seems to preclude any idea of the jaws of a dragon.

After the scene between Christ and Adam in Hell, Mary Magdalene begins to speak and the text gives the direction: *Magdelaine sus.* The word *sus* has heretofore been used in the directions of this play when an angel or angels are to sing as: *un ange chantet sus.* This evidently means that the angel is to sing *above* in Heaven and not on Earth where the action has been passing. But Mary Magdalene is on Earth.

Hence the *sus* points to the fact that she is not in Hell, where the action has been passing, but *above* Hell. Thus we seem to have a case in which Hell is represented on a level below the stage proper.

In the final play of the Jubinal collection, the *Résurrection,* Terrestrial Paradise, with the Tree of Life, is shown, but the scene was evidently on the stage proper and was distinct from Heaven. The devil speaking to Eve in Paradise says that if she will eat of the fruit she will be *lassus aux cieulx* with the angels. Also there is a stage direction: *Dieu voise entour le champ jusques Adam ait mengié du fruit.* This occurs during the scene in Paradise and the word *champ* which generally means the stage itself is evidence that the setting of this *Paradis terrestre,* as it is called by Adam, was not above the *champ* or stage. It is to be noticed that, after the descent into Hell, the ascent into Heaven is merely implied by the lines. This action, however, is common to all plays of the *Résurrection* and surely took place. The Heaven scene existed, but it was toward the scenes on Earth and in Hell that the eyes of the spectators were directed.

When Adam and Eve have been driven out of Paradise, Adam is directed to pretend to till the ground and Eve to spin. Then they enter Hell. The direction: *Adam, en enfer, die* again shows that the interior of Hell was visible. The entrance of Christ into Hell takes place as usual; but the lines still give no hint of the dragon's head. The words *portes de ceste maison* are still employed. As has already been seen in the *Nativité,* Limbo was the *premier estage d'enfer,* and the scene was set within and not outside of the gates of Hell. The same disposition of scenery occurs in this play. Christ says of the prophets in Hell:

> Y sont devers une partie
> Qui limbe est appelée et dicte.

Thus the idea is growing of a Hell divided into different scenes; and here we find the first step in the direction of a more complicated scene which will occur in a later *Résurrection.* As for the level of the setting, the line *R'alon-m'en en bisme parfont* may be pointed out as significant.

The other scenes, on Earth, are simple. The sepulchre is represented. The scene with the *espicier* demands merely properties such as ointment and scales. Pilate was probably seated in state; but Caiaphas and Annas are not dignified with chairs, for when their short rôles are finished they are directed to "go where they wish." This is practically an exit. Finally there is a garden in which stands a pine tree.

Such are the settings of these early plays. The advancement over the liturgical drama is plain. More elaborate scenery will be introduced; but any indoor stage cannot differ greatly from these we have been describing, nor will all plays show more complicated settings in the future. From this period on, the great open air spectacles exist; but stages with simple decorations such as these, and even simpler, exist side by side with the open air mystery.

CHAPTER VI

THE problem of stage decoration becomes somewhat different when the longer *Passions* are considered, such as the *Passion d'Arras,* which contains about twenty-five thousand lines. It is divided into *journeés* or acts, however. Thus the difficulty of mounting such a play was materially lessened by the fact that scenery could be changed. Only one *journée* need be considered at a time in attempting to reconstruct the appearance of the stage of this play, which is so important in the history of the French drama of this period. It is probably the work of Eustache Mercadé and is dated between 1402–1414. According to Roy, the great *Passions* of the north in the fifteenth century are derived, with few exceptions, from the

Passion d'Arras, either in the first or second degree.

It was suggested by Petit de Julleville[1] that the miniatures in the manuscript, still preserved at Arras, would elucidate many obscure points in the stage decoration, if they were examined closely. But it would be extremely hazardous to draw from these miniatures any conclusions which are not fully corroborated by the text. For example, the manuscript begins with the direction: " Here is the Trinity in Paradise, that is: God the father sitting on his throne and about him are the angels and archangels in great multitude. . . . The others are on their knees before God, with Pity, who holds a branch of olive in her hand. And Justice is on her right, who holds a sword in her hand. And with Pity on their knees are Beauty, Wisdom, and Charity." In the miniature corresponding to this direction, God is in the sky surrounded by angels, while below him are the figures called for, standing in a meadow. On the next page, although no change of scene is noted in the text, the same figures are shown; but they are standing on what appears to be a tiled floor,

[1] Les Mystères, vol. II, p. 416.

with a green and gold wall for a background. On page five, the scene still being in Heaven, the same figures are shown in the same position; but the background has changed to a landscape in which a castle stands. The tiled floor appears on the following page. God is again represented on the seventh page with a sky as background; but the angels are entirely missing. Thus the artist has forgotten his first setting. God was first seated in an arm-chair. Here he sits on a box-like arrangement. The architecture both of the stable and the temple changes from miniature to miniature. Beginning with page 232 the work is done by a different artist. Granted that these artists saw this play or some other produced, there is little to suggest a stage. The pictures seem to be fanciful creations of the imagination.

The well-known miniature of the Valenciennes mystery, which has been so often reproduced, also gives a somewhat erroneous impression of the stage. It would be impossible to set such a Paradise on the roof of one *maison;* yet Mortensen, evidently relying on this miniature as evidence, describes the typical Heaven as "an immense halo of gold which turns inces-

santly, and on the edges of which some angels
are floating. It is the Empyrean, the seventh
circle where God is sitting in the midst of the
blessed phalanxes." [2] There is no real evidence
that such a machine for representing Heaven
ever existed, placed as this is supposed to be,
over one room. The question arises as to where
were the organ and the many angels to find
room. As represented by the miniature such
a scene, with such proportions, is a physical im-
possibility. Even though, with modifications,
such a setting might be possible, the scene is not
entirely typical of the Middle Ages. Such
grandeur is found only in the fifteenth and sixteenth centuries on open air stages. Thus the
evidence of miniatures must be used with dis-
cretion. The Valenciennes play extended over
twenty-five days. The miniature reproduces
only a very small part of the scenery and is
more or less fanciful. Also, had the representation not been one which was out of the
ordinary, it is not probable that any attempt
to reproduce the stage would have been made.
Thus error arises from publishing this minia-

[2] Mortensen, le Théâtre français au moyen âge (traduit
par Philipot), Paris, 1903, p. 177.

ture either as a typical stage for the whole period or as the whole stage of this particular play.

In the *Passion d'Arras* Heaven contains God and the angels, as usual.   There were also means of causing a bright light to shine from the angles. During the second *journée* a cloud passes in which the voice of God is heard.   Such machines are indicative of the growing importance of the scene in Heaven.   It cannot be said, however, that, even in this mystery, Heaven is the predominating scene.   Terrestrial Paradise is again distinct from Heaven or else the following stage direction would be meaningless: *Cy emmaine Jhesus l'humain linage en paradis terrestre.*

As Heaven was above the stage, it would be natural to place Hell on a lower level.   This seems to have been the case in this play, for the lines often refer to Hell as below Earth. For example: *Lassus en terre où j'ay trouvé* (line 17691), is a line spoken in Hell.   While on the other hand we find the following lines spoken on Earth: . . . *entre où parfont d'infer* (line 21012); *Descendant où limbe d'infer* (line 22851); *Aux tenebres d'infer descendre*

(line 23134). There is little, if any, reason
for mistrusting this evidence. To place Hell
below the level of Earth is no more surprising
than to place Heaven above. In fact it would
be strange if this were not the case, in view of
the system of stage decoration which was in
vogue. It is unfortunate that there is no stage
direction in this play tending to prove that the
scenery was thus arranged; but whatever evidence is found, is favorable to the theory that
the stage consisted of more than two levels.

Hell itself is conceived as a stronghold. Its
entrance is a gate or doors, for the devils say:
Fremons noz portes à chainnies (line 18158)
and a stage direction: *Cy abat Jhesus les portes
d'infer,* carries out the same idea. There is a
miniature in the manuscript which represents
some devils issuing from the mouth of a dragon;
but there is also another which represents the
entrance of Hell as stone gates. Thus nothing
can be proved from these miniatures, even if
the theory of the influence of stage scenery on
art be accepted. These miniatures belong to the
latter part of the fifteenth century; and if they
prove anything, it is that the setting of Hell was
hesitating at that period between a dragon's

mouth and gates. The interior is evidently divided into Limbo, where Adam and the prophets are, and Hell proper in which Lucifer is chained in the flames. In addition to the gates, a window is implied in the line (20875): *Je viens de fermer no hucquiet (guichet).*

The scenes requiring a special setting for the first day are a *maison* for Joseph and Mary, a *maison* for Elizabeth the house of the *Evesque,* Herod's palace, an inn, the stable, the temple, a pastoral scene, the idols in an Egyptian temple, and at least a chair for Octavian. The Three Kings are as usual supposed to come from their kingdoms; but these are merely places on the stage and were probably without special scenery. Thus we may count ten different scenes at the most. There is no evidence of special setting for cities. The different scenes were quite elaborate. For example, the temple could be entered, an altar stood within, and in the action of the second day Christ is carried to the pinnacle of the temple. The palace of Herod had a door, and there were seats within the hall. The Three Kings go to bed at the inn, and the scene must have been carefully set. Line 1651 . . . *empres ce buisson* shows the nature of the pastoral scene.   There is also a tree which bows before Christ.

The second day or act required, first of all, the river Jordan.   The palace of Herod appears again, and a prison is needed.   In the third day the prison was raised in the air by divine power.   The temple and *une très haulte montagne* were used in the scene of the temptation.   The wood, to which line 7650 refers, was perhaps the pastoral scene of the first day or was a part of the mountain scene.   It is possible that a part of the river scene served for the pool.   The burial of Lazarus called for a *fosse*. The house of Simon was shown and the table for the Last Supper was set within.   A garden is needed.   There are also *maisons* for Caiaphas, Annas, Pilate, Zaccheus, Martha, and for *l'homme à la canne*.   It would be possible to use scenery twice in this act.   For instance, the house of Simon is not necessary to the action during the scene at the house of *l'homme à la canne*.   The same setting could be used for both. This was done in the liturgical drama.   It is not possible to prove that it was the case in this play; but it would be a natural proceeding and one which would lessen the difficulty of setting

8

a stage.   Granting that all these scenes were represented, the number of scenes is large but perfectly possible on an open air stage.   In the heading of one of the divisions of the play there is a *chastel* mentioned which is not needed in the action.   Thus we do not count this scene. The *chastel* where the ass is found is also left out of the reckoning for reasons already explained.[3]

The complicated scenes are the temple, Herod's palace, the prison, the house of Simon and the house of Zaccheus.   In both of these houses a table must be set.   The houses of Caiaphas, Annas, and Pilate might well have been chairs or thrones covered with a canopy.   The mountain and the river would also require a rather large space.   The other scenes, even the forest and the garden, would be easily set.   In addition to the above scenery a tree for Zaccheus, an elder tree, and a fig tree were shown.   Thus, if in reckoning the number of scenes consideration is taken of the fact that few were difficult, it is easily seen that such a stage is not impossible nor a matter of great wonder, even though it is curious.

[3] See p. 100.

For the third day the setting is much simpler. Pilate's *maison* is shown, and he also enters and comes out of a *prétoire*. Herod's palace still occupies its place. Jesus is bound to a pillar in the house of Caiaphas. This may well have been one of the supports of the canopy so often found over the chair of a high personage. The prison also remains. The words *ouvrez nous l'huis* of line 15457 refer to the house of the blacksmith, an important scene in the Passion Plays. The "very high mountain" of the preceding day has become Calvary. There is an "altar to an unknown god"; and lastly, the sepulchre.

The prison, the houses of Annas, Caiaphas, and Pilate are the scenes which occur again in the fourth day. The house of Joseph of Arimathea is implied in the words: *J'enterray ens.* In addition to the *maisons* the *Chastel de Maux* is seen. It is interesting to note that when the apostles close the doors of their house, the interior is still visible, for the stage direction says after this action: *Adonc mettent la table, et Jhesus mange en leur presence.* This is quite conclusive proof that the wall of the room toward the audience was taken out.[4]   A sea with

---

[4] See p. 219 for discussion of this point.

a ship is also necessary and the mountain is now Mount Olivet, a scene large enough to hold all the apostles. In this act *paradis terrestre* is again set as in the first day.

This is the scenery for the Passion of Arras when it was presented in its entirety. Nothing, however, would prevent giving a part of it, just as parts of the *Vieil Testament* were given at Paris. In either case the stage would not be overcrowded. Yet it did happen at Rouen in 1474 that the main stage was not made large enough to contain all the scenes, for, as we are told by the description of the stage in the manuscript, *les establies des six Prophetes estoient hors des autres en diverses places et parties d'icely Neuf Marchié.*

The main stage was set as follows:

Premierment vers Orient.

Paradis.

Ouvert faict en maniere de Throsne et reçons d'or tout autour. Au milieu duquel est Dieu en une Chaiere parée et au costé dextre du luy Paix et soubz elle Miséricorde; et au senestre Justice et soubz elle Vérité; et tout autour d'elles neuf ordres d'Anges les uns sur les autres.

Nazareth.
1. *La Maison des parens Nostre Dame.*
2. *Son Oratoire.*
3. *La Maison de Elizabeth en Montaigne.*

Hiérusalem.
1. *Le Logis de Symeon.*
2. *Le Temple Salomon.*
3. *La demeure des Pucelles.*
4. *L'Ostel de Gerson Scribe.*
5. *Le lieu du peuple Payen.*
6. *Le lieu du peuple des Juifz.*

Bethléem.
1. *Le lieu de Joseph et de ses deux Cousins.*
2. *La Crache ez Beufz.*
3. *Le lieu où l'en reçoit le tribut.*
4. *Le Champ aux Pasteurs contre la Tour Ader.*

Romme.
1. *Le Chasteau de Sirin Prévost de Syrie.*
2. *Le Temple Apollin.*
3. *La Maison de Sibille.*
4. *Le Logis des Princes de la Synagogue.*
5. *Le lieu où l'en reçoit le tribut.*
6. *La Chambre de l'Empereur.*
7. *Le Throsne d'icelluy.*
8. *La Fontaine de Romme.*
9. *Le Capitole.*

Enfer faict en maniere d'une grande gueulle se cloant et ouvrant quant besoing est.

Le Limbe des Peres faict en maniere de Chartre et n'estoient veus sinon au dessus du faux du corps.

Les places des Prophetes ez divers lieux hors les autres.[5]

[5] Frères Parfaict, vol. II, p. 494.

The prologue tells us that signs were used in this play to aid the spectators in recognizing the different scenes:

> Présent des lieux, vous les pouvez cognoistre
> Par l'escript tel que dessus voyez estre.

This means of marking scenery does not seem to have been employed often in France. The divisions of the scenery into cities carries out the theory that, as a general rule, there was no special setting to mark cities, such as is implied by the miniature in the Valenciennes mystery. The houses or palaces of a town were sufficient to represent the locality of the action when it changed from Rome to Jerusalem, for instance, without the aid of a gate or wall bearing the name of the place.

The remarkable point in this quite careful description is that no mention is made of Heaven being above Earth. All that is said is: *Premierment vers Orient. Paradis.*[6] The setting is noted, and Nazareth is mentioned as coming next on the stage. There is nothing to suggest that the houses in Nazareth were be-

[6] The abode of the blessed being toward the rising sun is a conception common to ancient as well as modern literature.

neath Heaven; on the contrary, the description
cannot be interpreted in any other way except
as meaning that all the scenes were on the same
level. The objection may be made that usually
there is no doubt that Heaven is above the stage.
Yet the writers of this period who take the
trouble to describe the setting at all, are so explicit concerning the scenery of Heaven and
take such care to inform us that it was above
Earth, that it is unlikely that this writer would
have failed to mention this fact had it been true,
for he is exact in noting the rest of the decoration. Only in considering the general rule of
placing Heaven on a higher level, does one become doubtful. But one of the points to be
insisted upon is that, from the very beginning,
a certain setting may have existed only once,
and the stage varied greatly according to the
imagination of the stage carpenters, the form
of the play, and the conditions under which it
was produced. This play, represented in the
open air on a large stage, may well have been
set on one level, because of the difficulty of placing so large a scaffolding as Heaven needed
above another scaffolding.

Heaven, placed at the eastern end of the

stage, is separated by all the rest of the scenery from Hell. The entrance of Hell is in the form of a dragon's mouth. This setting became popular in the fifteenth century. Had it been the general rule from the early plays down to these productions it would have been described before and taken as a matter of course rather than as a novelty at this period.[7]   Behind the dragon's head is found Limbo which is within Hell. Thus the devils evidently passed through the mouth of the dragon and again appeared before the eyes of the spectators instead of merely disappearing below the stage or behind the scenes when they entered Hell. If this were not the case, the scene in which Christ enters Hell and frees the prophets from Limbo could not be consistently acted, for he would be out of view if the dragon's head did not lead to Limbo.

Petit de Julleville has reckoned the number of *maisons* in this play as twenty-two, not counting Paradise, Hell and Limbo or the *établies*

---

[7] The first direct mention of this scene gives it as occurring in 1437 at Metz. *La bouche et entrée de l'enfer de icelluy jeu estait très bien faicte; car par ung engin, elle se ouvroit et reclooit seule quand les diables voulloient entrer ou issir.   Et avoit celle hure deux gros yeux d'acier* . . . Croniquer de Metz, ed. Huguenin, p. 201.

of the six prophets. But if we count the number of settings on the main stage we find the number to be nineteen. This number includes Paradise, Hell, and Limbo, but excludes such places as *le lieu du peuple Payen,* since they are not decorated with scenery. The *Oratoire* is also more of a property than a scene. The stage, therefore, could not contain more than nineteen or twenty scenes even though it was in the open air, for the rest of the scenery could not be arranged on it. Although there was no limit for the size of the stage out of doors, yet, since more than twenty *maisons* was a difficult setting at Rouen, it is possible that this number was rarely, if ever, exceeded even in these great provincial spectacles which occurred rarely and which must have been very curious to Parisians, who were accustomed to the indoor stages where such settings were impossible. It is true that the Parisian saw mimed mysteries on temporary stages in the open air; but the true Parisian stage was inclosed in a hall from the end of the fourteenth century onward.

The *Passion de Sémur,*[8] played in 1488, is an example of a play which stands midway be-

[8] Roy, *op. cit.*

tween the simple plays of the Jubinal collection
and the greater mysteries. It is imitated from
the *Passion de Ste. Geneviève* and a comparison
of the stage decoration of the two dramas will
show that the stage carpenters had a more difficult setting to construct in the later play.

The action begins in Paradise with God in
a chair and *Angeli hinc et inde.* There is nothing unusual in this; but an added touch of
realism is given when he bids that light be
created. This is represented by drawing back
a curtain. *Estolatur quedam cortina que
erit ante ipsum, et plene videatur a populo.*
This scene was on the customary higher level,
as is proved by the stage directions: *Hic as-
cendant paradisum* and *Modo descendat de
paradiso.* This was not the only level above the
stage, however. Terrestrial Paradise is below
and distinct from Paradise proper, for we read
in a stage direction: *Descendat de Paradiso et
vadat juxta paradisum terrestrem. . . .* But line
894 *En paradix terrestre en hault* is evidence
that this scene was not on the same level with
Earth, and this arrangement is fully carried
out by the rubric . . . *Et sic adscendant in
paradiso terrestre, et Anima Christus sedeat in*

quadam cathedra. This scene is set as an orchard, being called *Ce vergier* (line 546); and, of course, it contains the Tree of Life. Another of the trees is mentioned as a fig tree.

Hell is represented as usual. As God sits on his throne in Heaven, so Lucifer sits on his royal throne in Hell. The entrance of this scene does not appear to have been marked by a dragon's head. Line 8501: *Mort, fai que la porte soit close* and the direction: *Modo cadant porte inferni,* using the word *porte,* shows how the author conceived the scene in his imagination. The following lines also show that he thought of Hell as below Earth: *En bisme l'avons fait descendre* (line 456); *Que beaulcob d'ames cy descende* (line 1237); *Et cy viens en enfert descendre* (line 8687); *Je croy qu'elle vient de lassus* (line 5217). It would be strange if the author's idea were carried out only in regard to the elevations of Paradise and Terrestrial Paradise. Thus we evidently have a stage of four levels.

The action of the First Day needs quite a number of properties such as altars for Cain and Abel; an altar, a table and couch for Noah; a stone in the desert from which water gushes

forth at the command of Moses. The ark is
built or is rather supposed to be built on the
stage. The scene was exact enough to show the
one window, for a direction bids it be closed.
(*Hic claudat fenestram*). A carefully prepared scene is also shown as follows: *Hic debet
Deus descendere de paradiso in montem Sinay,
et introire domum[9] igneam subtiliter factam de
aqua vite, et ibi debet oculte bucina bucinare in
dicta domo ignea.*

An entr'acte is practically caused by the
long prophecies. The properties just mentioned
were not all necessary for the action which
follows. Are we to believe that they all held
their place on the stage and that even the ark
stood incongruously before the eyes of the spectator as he watched the birth of Christ? Or
would such scenery, which had served its purpose and would now be in the way, be quietly
removed? There is nothing to prove that the
stage was cleared; but this would be a natural
procedure, unless the producers of the play
were trying to embarrass themselves as much as
possible.

[9] The word *domum* evidently means ''place'' in this
indication as in others in this play. It does not refer
to a *maison*.

After the prophecies the action begins in the temple where there is an altar. The scene must have been well constructed because the devil is able to carry Christ *super pennaculum templi.* Later the devil carries Christ *super montem.* This was probably the same scene which served for Mt. Sinai earlier in the play. The house of Elizabeth is implied by line 2111: *Paix soit dedans ceste maison.* The scene is not very important to the action and was probably represented only in a summary fashion. The stage direction: *Modo vadat ad domum suam* would generally show a house for Mary; but since the word *domum* may mean merely " place " as it is used in the rubrics of this play, it is difficult to decide whether special scenery was employed for the house of Mary. The action could be understood without it. The house of Rusticus, however, is needed in both acts of this drama. The interior of the stable is naturally indispensable. Herod and Octavianus probably occupied thrones as usual and constitute two separate scenes. The Sibyl is directed as follows: *Recedet et intret cameram suam.* The river Jordan and a prison are two other well-known scenes which complete the setting for the First Day.

The stage for the Second Day is somewhat more complicated, Caiaphas, Annas, Herod, and Pilate probably occupy chairs; but the house of Simon is large enough for the Last Supper to take place within it. The temple appears again as does also the house of Rusticus. The actors sit down and eat in the house of Mary Magdalene. The tomb of Lazarus appears. (*Tunc sepeliunt Lazarum et ponunt in sepulcro.*) The mountain is again represented. The Garden of Olives is referred to by the words *Hic vadant,* and the action demands the usual ditch into which Peter throws himself. (*Intret in foveam.*) The *carceres* of the First Day is evidently the *turrim* in which *Barrabas* is confined in this act. *Tunc solvatur a columna* shows the usual action. A forge is also necessary as well as the tomb. After the descent into Hell, there are needed the chateau of Emmaus and the house in which Christ appears, *casi januis clausis.* One is again inclined to wonder whether some other scenery was not reused for these scenes. The stage direction: *Vadant omnes Judei in domum pontificis* may also point to a setting, the use of the word *domum* again being ambiguous. We thus have

another example of a play with quite a number
of scenes demanded at once, if it were given in
its entirety.   Yet even counting such scenes as
the tombs, the ditch, and the thrones of the high
personages the number is less than twenty, including Hell, Heaven, and Terrestrial Paradise.   No matter how many "places" were
shown, the number of real scenes is by no means
great, for it must be remembered that this stage
was undoubtedly in the open air and constructed
for the occasion.

CHAPTER VII

Different Levels in Hell in Michel's *Résurrection.*
Idea Derived from Greban's *Passion.* Description of the
scene in Hell. Terrestrial Paradise and Heaven Scenes
on Earth. Some Scenes in Michel's *Passion.*

THE *Résurrection,* attributed to Jean Michel
and played at Angers in 1471, furnishes a very
long and careful description of Hell, a scene
which must have been very complicated, since
different levels were used to indicate the degrees
of punishment. The source of this scene is
apparently in Greban's *Passion,* a work which
Michel must have known since his *Passion* is
an amplification of two *journées* of Greban's
Passion. The description of Hell given by
Lazarus in Greban's play is, as will appear
later, the model upon which Michel based his
scene. This account of Hell reads as follows:

> C'est ung abisme de destresse,
> ung hideux gouffre de tristesse
> ou toute misere survient.
>   Et puisque parler en convient,

sçavoir devez en ce party
que l'enffer total en ce vient
qu'il est en quatre pars party;
et comment qu'il soit depparty,
chacune des pars assés nuit:
ou enffer est peine s'ensuit.

   Et en la plus haulte partie
qui le limbe des peres est,
sont des prophetes . . . . .

   En l'aultre lieu qui est notoire
et bien ordonné par raison,
est l'enfer qu'on dit purgatoire.

. . . .

L'aultre enfer qui plus bas descent,
Ou les sieges sont mal ornés,
est lieu par tenebre indecent
et la sont les enffans morsnés.

. . . .

   Au plus bas est le hideux gouffre
tout de desesperance taint
ou sans fin art l'eternel souffre
de feu qui jamès n'est estaint.[1]

If this description be followed, Hell is divided into four levels. The highest is the Limbo of the Fathers;[2] below this is Purgatory which

---

[1] Mystère de la passion d'Arnoul Gréban publié . . . par G. Paris et G. Raynaud. Paris, 1878, lines 15791 ff.

[2] Cf. line 1225 of the prologue spoken from Hell *lassus ou limbe* . . . and lines 2369 ff. *hors du limbe . . . et mis en enffer au plus bas.*

is within Hell; Limbo of the infants comes next in order; the lowest of all is the pit of Hell. If these divisions be kept in mind, it will be seen that they correspond to the setting as Michel directed that it be arranged. Since the action and the scenery are so easily reconstructed, the play is here analyzed as an example of the open air drama of the period.

After a prologue, Peter and John begin the play with lamentations. Christ has been crucified and the three crosses with their victims are visible. The souls in Limbo sing. Enfer is personified and speaks; and Satan begins his rôle outside of Hell but he soon enters. Other devils appear and enter Hell. They are going to a council. *Icy cerberus crie à haulte voix dessus le portal d'enfer.* He is summoning the devils. *Icy viennent tous les dyables sur le portal devant tout le peuple.* They have come to the *parloer sur le portal d'enfer.* This is the accustomed place for councils to be held. If the Valenciennes miniature is correct in this detail, it is a kind of council chamber with barred windows. It occupies the upper part of the gate of Hell, which in this mystery does not seem to have been a dragon's jaws. Hell is a stronghold guarded by cannons, and its entrance seems to have resembled a city gate. Surely Michel would have mentioned the dragon, had he imagined it as appearing. He was so exact in details that he would hardly have overlooked such an important piece of scenery. When he does mention the entrance he says *portal* or *portes*. Why conjecture a dragon's head? Such a setting was not obligatory.

After a long council as to how to keep Christ from entering Hell, two of the devils go to the cross. The soul of Christ, clad in white, kneels near the cross facing Paradise, which is above the rest of the stage as usual. Christ prays with joined hands, and the angels descend to him. Mamouna, one of the devils, takes the soul of the bad thief, which is clad in a black shirt. Satan tries to keep Christ from descending into Hell. *Icy se doive faire pause et tous les dyables excepté sathan viennent tous à l'entree d'enfer et lors comme espouvantez feront signes amiratifz en mettant coullevrines arbalestes et canons par maniere de deffence. Et eulx estans sur le portal l'ame de jesucrist accompaignee de quatre anges et de l'ame du bon larron viendra aux portes d'enfer trainant*

apres elle sathan enchesné d'une chaine.   Then
the soul of Christ strikes, with his cross, the
gates, which are broken; and the soul enters
within Hell accompanied by the soul of the good
thief and the four angels.   Christ condemns the
devils; and, with the angels, he binds Satan
hand and foot and then places him on the
marche du puis d'enfer.   It is to be noted that
the action is taking place within Hell.   Thus
the interior of Hell was fully visible.   The gate
was therefore not facing the audience directly
but faced the stage, so that the scenery behind
could be in full view.

The soul of Christ throws Satan into the
pit and he cries most horribly.   *Et icellui puis
doit estre edifié iouxte le pallour de dessus le
portal d'enfer entre iceluy portal et la tour du
limbe par devers le champ du jeu pour myeulx
estre veu.*   This direction gives the exact place
of the pit and also shows that the *pallour* or
council chamber is not merely at the gate but
is above it.   The description is then carefully
continued.   *Et doit estre fait ledit puis en telle
maniere qu'il resemble par dehors estre mas-
sonné de pierres noires de taille.   Et si doit estre
si large qu'il y puisse avoir separacion entre les*

deux parties. En l'une desquelles parties soit
fait feu de souffre ou autrement saillant con-
tinuellement hors dudit puis. Et doit estre
fait par soufflez ou autrement subtillment qu'on
ne l'appercoive. Et en l'autre partie du puis en
laquelle sera jecté sathan n'aura point de feu
et s'en istra ledit sathan par une fenestre qui
sera faicte par devers enfer asses bas. Et apres
qu'il aura esté jecté, ledit feu doit jecter plus
grande flambe par avant. Et doit on tirer aucuns canons en ce faisant et avoir tonneaux
plains de pierres ou d'autres choses que l'en
doit faire tourner affin qu'ilz facent la plus horrible noise et tempeste que l'en pourrait faire.
Apres lesquelles choses ainsi faictes silence doit
estre imposee. Et alors l'ame de jesus doit rompre a force avec le bout de sa croix et avec le pie
la tour du limbe de laquelle tour la faczon sera
cy apres devisée. Notez que le limbe doit estre
au costé du parloer qui est sur le portal d'enfer
et plus hault que ledit parlouer en une habita-
tion qui doit estre en la fasson d'une grosse tour
quarree environnee de retz et de filetz ou d'autre
chose clere affin que parmi les assistens puis-
sent veoir les ames qui y seront quant l'ame de
jesus aura rompu ladicte porte et sera entree

dedens. Thus the large square tower of Limbo,
which is higher than the *parlouer* which itself
is above the gate, is on the highest level in Hell
just as it is described by Lazarus in Greban's
*Résurrection. Mais par avant la venue de
l'ame de jesus en enfer ladicte tour doit estre
garnie tout a l'environ par de hors de rideaux
de toille noir qui couvreront par dehors lesditz
retz et filetz et empescheront que on ne voye
jusques a l'entree de ladicte ame de jesus et
lors à sa venue seront iceulz rideaux subtillement tirez a costé tellement que les assistens
pourront veoir dedens la tour. Et notez que à
la venue de l'ame de jesus doit avoir plusieurs
torches et falotz ardans dedens ladicte tour en
quelque lieux qu'on ne les puisse veoir qui
feront grant clarté. Et derrière ladicte tour en
ung autre lieu qui ne puisse estre veu doit avoir
plusieurs gens crians et ullans horriblement
tous à une voix ensemble.*

Purgatory, as in Greban's play, is below
Limbo and within the gates of Hell. *Il est à
noter que le chartre de purgatoire doit estre au
dessoubs du limbe a costé, auquel doit avoir dix
ames sur lesquelles doit apparoir semblance
d'aucuns tourmens de feu artificiellement fait*

par eaue de vie. Et d'icelui purgatoire (evidently in the form of a prison) *l'ame de jesus rompra la porte pareillement a force et puis entrera dedens acompaigné desditz anges.— Icy endroit l'ame de jesus tire hors toutes les ames de purgatoire et les amaine avecques les autres ames du limbe des peres et doit avoir ung autre limbe deputé pour les petits enfans non circoncis et sans avoir eu remede contre le peche originel. Lequel limbe desdits petis enfans doit estre au dessoubz de celui des peres à costé.* . . . In Greban's description this part of Hell is placed below Purgatory as well as below the Limbo of the Fathers; but the two scenes practically correspond. In both, the Limbo for children comes after Purgatory. Greban then mentions the pit of Hell. Michel has already described this part of Hell because the action centered about it first. But surely Michel is directing that the scene be set according to Greban's description. Thus there was a stage of more than two levels.

The soul of Christ and the other souls remain in the towers of the Limbo of the Fathers. Then Caiaphas places the guards about the sepulchre.

When the discovery is made that the body is
gone, there are the usual scenes before Pilate
and Caiaphas, but no scenery is mentioned.
Joseph is summoned. *Joseph monte sur son
asne et va parler aux juifz.* Evidently live
animals were brought upon the stage. When
he dismounts he bids his servant to go back to
his *hostel*. This place is not important or necessary to the action, and was probably not marked
by scenery. The line is merely a makeshift
to have the ass led away by the servant. Joseph
is condemned to prison, and a carpenter and a
mason build the prison in view of the audience.
Joseph is locked in, and the keys are removed.
The Jews go to their place on the stage, showing that their part is finished for the time being.
To go to one's *place* or *lieu* was practically an
exit. Gabriel comforts Notre Dame; then he
returns *divers le hault paradis jusqua ce qu'il
soit envoyé oster la pierre de dessus le tombeau.*
The three Marys go to the apothecary whose
shop is probably shown by his wares. They
return to Notre Dame and the first act is over.

When the action begins again, the soul of
Christ and the other souls are still within Limbo;
and Gabriel is directed "to have mounted"

into Paradise where he was when the action closed on the day before. The soul of Christ, accompanied by the three angels, Saint Michel, Saint Uriel, and Saint Raphael, takes the soul of Adam by the hand, and Adam takes his wife by the hand and so on up to the last one. Christ then leads them out of Hell *dedens le champ droit en paradis terrestre.* This Terrestrial Paradise is a separate scene and is differentiated from the *hault paradis* on the stage, for the direction continues: *Et ce pendant gabriel doit estre ou hault paradis pour descendre quant jesus resucitera pour oster la pierre de dessus le tombeau.* Heaven therefore is above Terrestrial Paradise. The setting of this scene is described as follows: *Icy l'ange seraphin garde paradis terrestre et a vestements de rouge et visaige rouge tenant une espee toute nue en sa main et parle à l'ame du bon larron par ung carneau du mur endroit ledit guichet de paradis terrestre. Et icelui paradis doit estre fait de papier au dedens duquel doit avoir branches d'arbres les ung fleuriz les autres chargés de fruits de plusieurs especes comme cerises poires pommes figues raisins et telles choses artificiellement faictes et d'autres*

*branches vertes de beau may et des rosiers dont
les roses et les fleurs doivent exceder la haulteur
des carneaux et doivent estre de frais couppez
et mis en vaisseau[s] plains d'eaue pour les tenir
plus freschement.* The scene has not changed
much in two hundred years since the *Adam*
play was produced.

The cities are probably marked by the *maisons* supposed to be in them. For example,
John goes to the apostles *estans en jherusalem
en ung autre maison que celle du cenacle ou
est la mere de jesus et assez loing.* Peter is not
with the rest, but is in *une fosse du jeu.* These
are usual scenes; but the following directions
show a new departure for the stage in the shape
of trap doors and underground passages. *Lors
l'ame de jesus et celles de carinus et leonicus
se doivent partir de paradis terrestre et aler
visiblement devant les gens du jeu se bouter es
lieux ou sont les corps et y entrer sans les ouvir
pour resusciter . . . apres ladicte resurrection
faicte s'en doivent lesdictes troys ames aler par
soubz terre.* Magdalene and the other women
leave with their boxes and ointments, but they
*sejournent en chemin secretement jusques à ce
qu'il soit temps d'aler en avant. Et jesus vestu*

*de blanc accompagné de troys anges c'est assavoir
michel raphael et uriel doit soudainement et
subtillement saillir de dessoubz terre de costé
de son tombeau par une petite trappe de boys
couverte de terre laquelle se reclost sans qu'on
s'en apperçoive et se doit seoir sur son tombeau
sans le froisser ne entamer aucunement. Et
lors semblablement carinus et leonicus vestus de
blanc et les pieds nudz se sourdent et se resus-
citent de leurs tombeaux qui doivent estre en
jherusalem asses loing du tombeau de jesus
lequel doit estre hors de jherusalem. Et lors
soit fait artificiellement ung escroix terrible et
ung tremblement de terre dont les quatre gardes
du sepulchre cheent comme morz. . . .* After
the scene at the tomb, Christ " goes a little about
the stage," then disappears underground to appear to his mother, when the time comes, who
is alone in the house of the *cénacle.* Larinus
and Leonicus also disappear in the same way
to appear later to *Nycodemus* who is *en jherusalem en sa maison.* From this house the same
characters go underground to appear in the
house of Mary and Martha in Bethany. Thus
the stage must have been honeycombed beneath
with passages and trap doors. In this act

Joseph of Arimathea is given a house, and the same scene may have occurred during the action of the preceding day, although it is not mentioned in the first part of the play and is not necessary until now. Such questions would probably occur to the stage carpenters at the time and would be decided according to existing conditions. If the stage were not crowded, such a scene would probably remain throughout the play. If it were troublesome to mount, it would occur only when necessary. The *ostel* of Caiaphas must have been carefully set, for the two scribes place the four chevaliers *en divers lieux en l'ostel de cayphe soubz ung huys fermant à clef.* The same scene undoubtedly occurred in the first act, for there are scenes before Caiaphas.

A *maison* is required for *Jacques le mineur* when Christ goes *par dessoubz terre* to appear to him. This may have been one of the other *maisons* already noted which was free at this period of the action. Jesus appears to Joseph *en prison ou il est sans remuer ne rompre ladicte prison l'en doit tirer par contrepois, qui ystra par dessoubz terre, icelle prison et puis sera rassise comme devant.* Jesus takes Joseph

by the hand and leads him to the city of Arimathea which is probably figured by the house of
Joseph.   Christ disappears under ground and
goes to Jerusalem, where a council is held by
the Jews, first before Caiaphas and then before
Pilate.   Cleophas and Lucas go to *Emaux* where
they sit down at the table.   Christ appears before them, but *adonc jesus s'evanouist de leurs
yeulx subitement par ung engin.*   The *ostel
d'Emaux* being a time-honored scene from the
liturgical drama on, it was surely represented
by special scenery.   Lucas and Cleophas return
on the run to Jerusalem and enter the house
where the apostles are.   *Icy endroit thomas s'en
doit aler dehors et jesus entre par dessoubz terre
en la maison ou sont les disciples en jherusalem
leurs portes closes quant thomas s'en est alé.*
This is proof that the wall of a *maison* toward
the audience was taken out or else the action
could not have been seen.   After Christ has appeared in Terrestrial Paradise where he re-
ceives the homage and thanks of the prophets,
he is directed to go *en lieu secret* until it is time
for him to appear to his mother.   This is an
example of a real exit.   A comic scene between
a blind man and his servant ends the second

act, for the text says that the "blind man and his *varlet* go away as if going to drink and thereupon everyone ought to depart."

The Third Day is remarkable for its realistic setting for the sea. Seven of the apostles enter a boat on the sea. This is a scene which often occurred; but in this scene real water seems to have been employed, for the direction reads: *Icy saint pierre se vest et va par dessus une plance de boys laquelle doit estre atachee en l'eaue qu'on ne la voye et semble qu'il aille par dessus l'eaue.*

There are two mountains represented: *la montaigne de thabor* and the *mont d'olivet lequel doit estre soubz paradis.* The *maison du cenacle* is also placed under Paradise—the Paradise into which the ascension is made— Terrestrial Paradise, which is above the stage but is evidently not as high as the *hault Paradis.* If both scenes had been on the same level they would hardly have been differentiated by this expression. The souls from Hell were placed in Terrestrial Paradise, and thus the resurrected souls would also be placed there. Heaven is therefore divided into these two parts on two levels. Terrestrial Paradise has been fully described.   The *hault paradis* probably was the highest point where God sat enthroned above nine tiers of angels as was customary.

The ascension was managed as follows: . . . *et soit jesus vestu de blanc duquel il aura esté vestu quant il aura fait sa premiere apparucion à sa mere et si doit avoir ces V playes fort taintes de rouge en son costé dextre et ses piedz et mains lequel avecques les troys anges c'est assavoir gabriel raphael et uriel sera tiré apart le premier tout en faux et les deux fils symeon resuscités et les XLIX qu'il menra monteront secretement en paradis par une voye sans qu'on les voye mais leurs statures de papier ou de parchemin bien contreffaictes jusques au dit nombre L et ung parsonnages seront atachez à la robe de jesus et tirés amont. . . . Icy endroit doit descendre grant brandon de feu artificiellement fait par eaue de vie et doit visiblement descendre en la maison du cenacle sur nostre dame et sur les femmes et apostres qui alors doivent estre assis, et tant come il descendra se doit faire ung tonnoire d'orgues au cenacle et qu'il soient gros tuyaulx bien concors ensemble et en doulceur sur chascun d'eulx doit choir une langue de feu ardant dudit brandon et seront XXI en nombre. . . .*

The stage directions speak for themselves.
Their presence in such number and the care
with which they describe minute details show
the point to which the art of stage decoration
has risen. It is the scenery which furnishes
the interest of the play. Stage-setting is a delight to the eye and a wonder to the mind. It
is no longer a mere aid to the understanding.
Other machines may be introduced and more
scenes may be set at once; but the realism of
this scenery and the care with which it was set
on its several levels cannot be surpassed. The
scenes in Heaven and Hell are now the most
important from the point of view of scenic effect. The stage must have been very large, for
the scene of Paradise alone had to have space
for much scenery and many characters, and
only on an out-door stage would such a scene
be possible. Let us not believe that this stage,
with different levels, was the type of stage of
the Middle Ages. This is merely one of the
many ways that stages appeared. It was, in
some ways, the triumph of scenic art; but let
it be remembered that this great stage spectacle
disappears from view in the next hundred years
and that the simply decorated comic stage is in

reality of more importance in the history of the theater.

The decoration of the stage of Michel's *Passion* does not differ materially from the stages of the *Passions* already described. There is the same exactness in the scenery. The temple shows a quite careful construction with fifteen steps leading up to it. In the First Day— which is in reality the somewhat altered *Con- 'ception* by Greban—Reuben speaks as follows:

> Il fault quinze degrez monter,
> Devant que nul ait la notice
> Du grant autel de sacrifice.

A miracle is then performed by the child Mary walking up these steps. *Icy met marie sur le premier degré et monte seulle iusques au coupeau.* As in other plays Christ and Satan mount to the pinnacle of the temple, and the following direction explains how this was man- aged: *Icy se met jesus sur les espaules de sathan et par ung soudain contrepoys sont guindés tous deux sur le temple.* In the interior of the temple stand an altar and chairs. Joachin is directed to be *Devant l'autel du temple à genoulx;* and the doctors *s'en vont au temple seoir en haultes chaires.*

The birth of Christ takes place in the stable, and the angels *respandent grant lumière.* Also they are on a cloud: *Icy fault une nuee ou seront les anges.* The star shines, but *icy se absconse l'estoille.* It finally comes in view again and *se arreste l'estoille sur la maison.* Thus has this action grown since, in the liturgical drama, the star hung suspended on a string. But, as in the liturgical drama, chairs are still used for some of the actors: *Icy s'en vont ses trois personnaiges en leurs sieges.*

Another piece of stage business which has not occurred before takes place when Christ, accompanied by three apostles, climbs Mount Tabor. *Icy entre jesus dedens la montaigne pour soy vestir d'une robe la plus blanche que faire se pourrat et une face et les mains toutes d'or bruny et ung grant soleil a rays bruny par derriere puis sera levé hault en l'aer par ung soubtil contre pois et tantost apres sortira de la dicte montagne helye en habit de carme et ung chapeau de prophete a la teste et moyse d'autre costé qui tendra les tables en sa main et ce pendant parlera la magdaleine.* After the transfiguration *descent une clere nue sur jesus.*

The city of Jerusalem seems to have been marked not only by the *maisons* within it but also by a gate. *Icy s'arrestent tous ung peu loing de la porte de jherusalem.* This is a long advance in scenery over the chair of the liturgical drama which was *quasi* Jerusalem.

A special scene was also erected for the judgment of Christ by Pilate. *Icy vient pylate dedens le pretoire. Et est à noter qu'il y a au milieu du jeu ung parquet tout clos en carré et dedens ce parquet il y a une chaire haulte bien paree et une seconde chaire et en ceste seconde chaire se siet pylate pour faire le proces de jesus et ne se siet point a la haulte chaire jusques ad ce qu'il donne sa sentence contre jesus pour le crucifier. Item est a noter que dedens le parquet qui est le pretoire n'y a que pylate assis en la seconde chaire et jesus devant lui lyé par le corps et par les bras de cordage et tous les juifz sont dehors du pretoire assez loing.*

After the crucifixion there is an earthquake and *le voille du temple se rompt par le milieu et plusieurs morts tous ensevelis sortiront hors de terre de plusieurs lieux et iront deça et dela.*

Michel, therefore, wrote his plays with a

stage in mind which was to show several levels.
Perhaps the well-known description of the
theater at Angers in which his *Passion* was
played can be explained in the light of these
plays. The stage is described as consisting of
*cinq eschaffautz à plusieurs étages, couverts
d'ardoises, et que le paradis, qui était le plus
élevé,*[3] *contenait deux étages.* This citation was
taken by Morice[4] from the Frères Parfaict who
in turn claim to have gained this information
from *M. Poquet de Livonniere, Secrétaire de
l'Académie Royale d'Angers.*[5] The *Passion* to
which reference is made was given in 1468; but
unfortunately the stage decorations of this play
are not very explicit in regard to the number of
levels. The passage applies perfectly, however,
to Michel's Resurrection given at Angers in
1471. Paradise, as has been shown above, was
divided into two scenes: Terrestrial Paradise
and that part designated as the *hault paradis*
and hence above Terrestrial Paradise. This
corresponds to the above description exactly.
Earth naturally made another level; and Hell

[3] See Cohen's explanation, *op. cit.,* p. 78.

[4] Morice, Histoire de la mise-en-scène depuis les mystères jusqu'au Cid, p. 44.

[5] Note, vol. II, p. 290.

contained scenes on different elevations.   This
is probably what is meant by *plusieurs étages*.
Because the passage may be interpreted literally
in regard to the *Résurrection* in 1471, one has
no hesitation in believing that it was also true
that the scenery of the *Passion* in 1468 was also
on several elevations which gave the appearance
of *étages*.   The mistake lies not in trusting this
description in regard to Michel's plays in the
open air at Angers, but in assuming that scenery
was so constructed as a rule.   There are other
stages of more than two levels; but not all
stages were divided into *étages*.   The open-air
stage was most elastic; and the fact that a certain
arrangement of scenery existed at one performance in one place is no sure sign that other
stages were thus set as a rule, or, indeed, that
this arrangement ever existed a second time.

Exactly the opposite view is taken by Petit
de Julleville[6] in discussing the plan of the setting of a *Passion* published by Mone.[7]   This
plan shows an oblong stage with scenes set on
both sides of it.   There was no front nor rear
of the stage, the spectators being on both sides

[6] Petit de Julleville, *op. cit.*, vol. I, p. 392.

[7] Mone, Schauspiel des Mittelalters, p. 156.

of the platform. The neutral ground was thus between the two rows of scenes; and Mone believes that the *maisons* were without walls in order to allow a free view of the stage. This plan applies to a German Passion of the fifteenth century; but Petit de Julleville says in regard to this setting, that the stage decoration of the mysteries was the same throughout Europe in the Middle Ages. This is true only in a modified way. In fact, the variability of the setting from time to time and from place to place is remarkable. Thus in dealing with a plan of a stage, one must be careful not to generalize too broadly from it. This arrangement, awkward as it is, without doubt existed in Germany and may have existed in France. The setting of the liturgical drama may have taken this form when placed in the nave of a church; but it is to be remembered that the *Adam* play had a church for a background and could therefore hardly admit of this method. The prologues seem to name the scenes as if they extended in a straight or possibly curved line, but only showed one side to the audience. Surely this was true of scenery in an inclosed theater.

In front of this scenery was the neutral

ground upon which parts of the play were acted which required no scenery, such as cross-roads and battlefields. The rest of the action took place within the *maisons* where it was supposed to happen. We have no hesitation in making this categorical statement after having examined the plays. There are constant references in the lines to exits and entrances. The plays just examined contain stage directions showing that the *maisons* are to be used by the characters and are not for mere decoration. The existence of such scenes is evidence in itself that the action was carried on within them. Had it been otherwise, had the audience been accustomed to watching the action on neutral ground, scenery would not have developed as it did.[8]

[8] For editions of Michel's works Petit de Julleville,*op. cit.*, vol. II, p. 439 and p. 446 should be consulted.

CHAPTER VIII

Setting of Provençal Plays. Stage of Three Levels.

THE Provençal mysteries[1] throw light upon
many points of stage decoration and bring evidence which corroborates that furnished by the
northern mysteries. The mystery of the *Creation and the Fall* shows the division of the
two scenes of Paradise. God takes Adam and
Eve by the hand and leads them into *Paradise
terrestre. Aras s'en ane Dieu lo payre en Paradis.* This is a second Paradise or Heaven, for
when Adam and Eve have eaten of the Tree of
Life (*l'albre de vida*) and have fled under a
fig tree, then God descends from Paradise and
goes to Terrestrial Paradise (*verdier*) which is
on a lower plane. (*Dieu lo payre davale de
Paradis he s'en ane al verdier.*) This play
does not show that Terrestrial Paradise was
above the stage proper, but the *Jugement*

[1] Mystères Provençaux du quinzième siècle. Jeanroy et
Teulié. Toulouse, 1893.

Général of this collection gives evidence of such an arrangement.

Each actor had his place on the stage as in the northern mysteries, and there was sometimes a real exit for the purpose of changing costume. Thus in the *Jugement de Jésus:* the judges, counsellors, etc., *se devo partir del escadaffal he se devo anar abilhar en lo secret, cascun segon son abilhamen; he après devo venir cascun en son loc, he quant seran asetiatz. . . .* Lights can also be changed in these representations, for in another play we read: *Aras aprop que las tenebras son fachas.* Morice believed that darkness and light were made by lowering and raising gauze curtains, as water is represented to-day in the *Rheingold.*[2] Torches may also have been used. Such scenes would not be difficult in a closed theater, but must have been more or less failures in the open air. In the *Assomption de la Vierge,* when light is needed, the direction occurs: *et doit-on jecter flambées par dessoubz.*[3]

Gates instead of a dragon's head seem to have been the setting of Hell in the Provençal *Resur-*

[2] Morice: *op. cit.,* p. 115.
[3] Petit de Julleville, les Mystères, vol. II, p. 471.

rection.   When Christ is to enter Hell the stage direction says: *Aras Sant Miquel he Gabriel s'en ano an Jhesus dava (n) t los enfernis.*   Then Lucifer speaks from within.   The line: *Ubretz vos, portas infernals,* describes the entrance. There is a short scene in Hell which had to exist through the very nature of the plot.   Thus the interior of Hell must have been visible just as was the interior of Paradise, although gates served as an entrance.   (*Aras se ubrisquo las portas de paradis. . . .*)

The *Jugement Général* of this Provençal collection shows a stage of three levels.   The scene is carefully described.   *Et primo Nostre Senhor deu estre asetiat en una cadieyra ben parada he deu mostrar totas sas plaguas, en presentia de totz, totas dauradas.   He après hy deu aver quatre angiels, dos de cascun costat: que la hun porte la crotz, he l'autre lo pilar he la corda liada an lo pilar he l'autre los clavels he los foetz, he l'autre la lansa he l'esponsia.   He hy deu aver una cadieyra ben parada per asetiar Nostra Dama, quant sera hora, al costat drech de son filh.*   (We learn from a later direction that, before this time, Notre Dame is to be *en sa cambra tota sola en sa cadieyra. . . .*)   *He hy*

deu aver dos angi(e)ls, cascun an sa trompeta,
he en paradis deu estre Sant Miquel he gran cop
de angials anb el. *He los Sans devo estre a*
l'autre escadafal (evidently not in Paradise)
cascun en son loc, ordenatz an bancz. *He deu*
portar Sant Piere sa tiera coma papa, he los
emperados he reis segon lor estat, habilhatz
segon lor esse las vestimentas, qui verdas, qui
negras, qui an mosa. *He i aura emperadors,*
reys, he d(e) glieza, he femnas abilhatz segon
lor esse; los Juzieus seran ense(n)ble he los
autres aitant be, he venran quant seran apelatz
per los angials. *Los demonis seran a part, quant*
seran vengutz de infern, he seran devant Dieu
eternal he auran aguda lor centensia. *Nostra*
Dama tota sola sera en son loc irquamen abilhada
en lo escadafal gran, he estara aqui tro que sera
hora de venir. (*Escadafal gran* probably means
stage proper in distinction from the scenes
above.) *Justicia he Misericord(i)a he Vida*
seran totas ensemps sus lo escadafal gran. *La*
Mort sera en son loc sur lo escadafal. *Los*
Juzieus seran a part a l'escadafal gran, coma
so: Melchisedec, Aymo, Lamec, Zorobabel. *Los*
ydolatres seran a part sus lo escadafal, coma so:
Abiatar, Salatiel, Piqua-ausel, Talhafer, he

*d'autres. Lo malvatz crestias seran a part coma
los autres coma so: Symon, Aniquet, Mella,
Amon he los autres. Los religioas bernardins,
carmes, auguistis, predicadors, cordelies, meno-
retas coma so: Nason, Mathatias, Semey, Ami-
nadas, Balam, Hobet.*

Paradise is above the stage as is proved by
the direction: *Aras s'en davalo los angials a
l'escadafal. . . .* One goes to one end, the
other to the opposite end. They are also directed to *mount* into Paradise: . . . *he après,
quant s'en seran montatz en paradis, los mortz se
levaran, los huns dels tombels he los autres de
locz segretz, he venran totses davant Dieu he
se metran de ginolhos sans dire mot. Haprès
los salvatz s'en montaran en hun escadafal plus
bas que paradis, a la part dextra.* Thus Paradise is above all, but there is a kind of Terrestrial Paradise above the rest of the stage
not as high as the other Paradise. The damned
souls are naturally on the lowest level, and on
the other side of the stage: *he los dapnatz
demoraran al gran scadaffal, a la part senestra.*
This arrangement of the stage with the blessed
and the damned at opposite ends is not unusual.[4]

[4] See pp. 90, 118.

At least the exterior of Hell was represented on the stage, for when the trumpet has sounded Lucifer speaks *dedins sans hubrir la porta;* but the interior does not appear to have been visible. The damned enter Hell wailing and groaning. Then Hell closes. The saints mount into Paradise singing.

CHAPTER IX

Pantomimes of the Fifteenth Century. Their Influence on the Indoor Stage.

THE tableaux and pantomimes in which scenes from mysteries and miracles were represented continued to be produced throughout the fifteenth century. At the entrance of Charles VI. and Henri V. into Paris in 1420 there was made *un moult piteux mistere de la passion e Nostre Seigneur au vif* as it is represented about the choir of the cathedral of Notre Dame. The scaffolding or stage was about a "hundred paces long." [1] At the entrance of the duc de Beaufort in 1424 we learn from the same source that the mystery was represented as if the images were "nailed against the wall." When there was no action, the scenery must have been carefully set in order to make the story plain. The mere existence of such scenery before the eyes of the people must have had some effect

[1] Journal d'un bourgeois de Paris, Tuety. Paris, 1881, par. 291.

on the real stage of the period in making the scenery more sumptuous. A public accustomed to such sights would demand something more than a mere summary representation of places. The taste for great spectacles was fully aroused; and it was satisfied, although stages had to be constructed in the open air to allow the scenes of almost unbridled fancy to be carried out.

Not only were mysteries produced, but also allegorical scenes and scenes from miracle plays were mounted. In 1431, when Henry VI. entered Paris, the *mistere depuis la conception Notre Dame jusques Joseph la mena en Egypte* was given before the *Hôpital de la Trinité* where the *confrérie de la Passion* was established. It would be interesting to know how much scenery was taken from within this theater and set outside for the occasion; and how much, constructed anew for this special performance, was used afterward within the theater. The stage of the pantomime extended *depuis ung pou par-delà Saint Sauveur jusques au bout de la rue Ernetal.* No such spacious stage was possible within the *Hôpital de La Trinité* whose dimensions are

given as 21½ × 6 *toises.*[2]   Thus the number of
scenes represented at one time would be lessened
when the same mystery was given within doors,
either by cutting certain scenes or by changing
scenery.   But since the *confrérie* was probably
the producer of this mystery—it being given
before its theater—the influence of the silent
mysteries on the spoken mysteries is plain to
be seen.

At this same entrance the legend of St. Denis
was given at the *Porte S. Denis;* and the *seraines du Ponceau Saint Denis* attracted much
attention.   *Car là avoit trois seraines moult
bien ordonnées; et ou milieu avoit ung lis qui
par ses fleurs et boutons gectoit vin et lait . . .
et dessus avoit ung petit bois ou il y avoit
hommes sauvages qui faisoient esbatemens en
plusieurs manières et jouoient des escus moult
joieusement.*   There was also a "hunt for a
live deer most pleasant to see."   At the Châtelet
the allegorical scene of the bed of Justice was
exhibited.[3]

More of such scenes were exhibited in 1437
at the entrance of Charles VII.   *Devant le*

[2] See p. 192 for discussion of these figures.
[3] Journal d'un bourgeois, par. 589 ff.

Chastelet estoit un grand Rocher et Terrasse couvert d'un Boccage et pastis agréable où estoient les Pastoureaux avec leurs brebis . . . et audessous l'Arcade dudit Rocher estoit un Lict de Justice . . . et contre les Boucheries estoient représentez le Paradis, le Purgatoire, et l'Enfer.[4] The same scene is described by Enguerrand de Monstrelet showing that the pastoral scene is the annunciation made to the shepherds by an angel.[5] He also adds that the scene set *contre la boucherie* was the Judgment, and that St. Michel was weighing the souls.

Jean Chartier in his Chronique de Charles VII.[6] reports many scenes at the entrance into Gand of Monseigneur de Bourgogne in 1458. The first, which had a real setting, was a "garden or orchard in which there was a young girl about ten years old." The return of the prodigal was represented. Cicero was seen pleading before Cæsar, who was surrounded by twelve senators. *Dedens ladite porte eult ung autre eschaffault, et ou melieu avoit une fontaine et à l'environ l'estat de l'Eglise triumphant.*

[4] Frères Parfaict, vol. II, p. 171.
[5] Edition Buchon, vol. VI, p. 357.
[6] Edition of the Bibliotèque elzévirienne, vol. III, p. 81 ff.

11

Unfortunately this last scene is not described. Near this was a shepherd who has collected his strayed sheep. The river was cleverly utilized for the scene of Christ walking on the water, and " St. Peter wishing to go to Our Lord . . . and seeing himself in danger of being drowned " *dist par escript: Domine salvum me fac.* Almost every scene had some such explanatory motto, especially the figures of the prophets which occurred at intervals. An extensive scene was one of a *forteresse à deux tournelles à deux carreaulx* at the door of which stood a giant, Mars, and beside him was a lion. In front of the fortress there was a wood, in which there were dragons, wolves, foxes, etc., which seemed to wish to enter the stronghold. *Et estoit devant ladite porte ung homme représentant les trois Estatz de mondit seigneur, c'est assavoir sur la teste comme homme d'Eglise, du costé dextre d'une robbe longue de drap de soye, le costé senextre comme laboureur des champs.* There was also an elephant *portant ung chasteau* on which were two men and four children singing. In all there were eighteen scaffoldings.

There were also different levels in the setting of these pantomimes, for in 1484 at the entrance of Charles VIII. into Paris the following arrangement is noted by an anonymous chronicler as having been made at the Châtelet:

> Il y avoit un grand Eschaffaut,
> Oú illec un Roy se séet
> Par dessus les autres, au plus haut.[7]

The same document recounts that Judas was seen hanged on a tree. *Donc en Enfer il descendit.* If this latter action was visible the spectators must have seen Hell on a lower level.

Going out of France for the moment we find at Antwerp, in 1494, an ingenious scene in which was *un chasteau pendant en aer, de six à sept pieds de hault, et aultant de large, lequel, par sublilité d'engiens, mena moult et horrible bruict.*[8]

The entrance of Marie d'Angleterre in 1514 was an occasion for several novel allegorical scenes. On one scaffolding was a *grand Navire d'argent voguant sur la mer.* The ship must have been of good size for in it were found Bacchus, a queen, sailors, etc. At the four corners of the sea the winds were personified in the shape of four *grands Monstres soufflans.*

[7] Frères Parfaict, vol. II, p. 177.

[8] Chroniques de Jean Molinet, vol. V, p. 14, éd. Buchon.

At the *Fontaine du Ponceau* there was a garden
within which stood a lily and a red rose bush.
At the Châtelet, Justice and Truth were descending from the celestial throne upon Earth;
and on the right and the left were the *douze
Paris de France.*

Again in 1517 in Paris, we find different
levels existing. At the entrance of Queen
Claude there was an *Eschaffaut et au plus haut
estoit un Ciel clos et par dessus une nuée,
laquelle s'ouvroit, dont sortoit une Colombe.*
Another scaffolding was surmounted by a sun
within which stood Charity. Below her were
five goddesses, and below them were ten persons
including the pope and the emperor.[9]

Thus these spectacles continue even down to
the seventeenth century. Their influence on
out-door spoken mysteries has already been rec-
ognized; but at the same time the influence
must have been reciprocal. When the *confrérie*
represented a pantomime or tableaux in front
of the theater they naturally took at least some
of their scenery with them. Petit de Julleville calls attention to the fact that allegorical
scenes became common in the latter part of the

[9] Frères Parfaict, vol. II, p. 191 ff.

fifteenth century and that their object was to
flatter some powerful person.   In the *Jeu de la
Feuillée* we saw an allegorical scene in the shape
of the Wheel of Fortune, thus these scenes were
not foreign to the stage.   Yet, just as the Passion Play was influenced by these tableaux, so
undoubtedly the miracle and morality plays
owed something in their stage decoration to such
scenes as those recorded above.   The morality
depended much upon costumes; and costumes
played a large part in these shows which also
served to keep aroused the taste for realism,
exactness and finally, elaborateness of scenery
which characterize the scenery of the late
Middle Ages and Renaissance.   All kinds of
scenes were presented on a large scale from the
scenes in the life of *Renart* to the crucifixion.
Thus the whole theater, religious and comic,
must have felt this influence in some degree;
but the religious stage felt it most strongly,
especially when constructed out of doors when,
in spite of the prodigious length, the scenery
not "the play is the thing."

CHAPTER X

Stage of the *Vie de Saint Martin* on Three Levels. Number of Scenes. Settings of Other Miracle Plays of the 15th Century. Comparison of these Plays with the *Miracles de Notre Dame*. Miracles of the 16th Century. A Stage on One Level. The Use of the Dragon's Head. The *Actes des Apôtres*.

THE early miracle plays, as has been seen, demanded a stage of two levels; but the setting of the Hell scene became more and more popular, and in the *Vie de Saint Martin*[1] an example is found of a miracle play which not only demands a scene in Hell, but also evidently disposes its scenery on three levels. The prologue gives the setting of the stage as follows:

> Premier voilla en hault assis
> Jesuchrist en son paradis,
> Et la doulce vierge Marie,
> Les anges en sa compaignie,

[1] Le Mystère de la vie et hystoire de monseigneur sainct Martin. Collection de Poesie, Romans, Chroniques etc. publiée d'après d'anciéns Manuscrits et d'après les editions des XV⁰ et XVI⁰ siècles. Paris.

Sainct Pierre et sainte Cecille
Saincte Agnes qui est bien habille.
Et voicy le roy de hongrie,
Chevaliers en sa compaignie
Son filz martin est pres de luy,
Et la prince de la ioste luy.
Cestuy qui est en cest arroy
Si est le messagier du roy.
Voyez cy prestre en leur chappelle,
Qui leur semble bonne et belle.
Icy est la maison du prince,
Qui est seigneur de la province;
Ses chevaliers sont la dedans
Et grant partie de ses gens.
    Sa est le conte de millan,
Sa femme o luy sans ahan,
La soeur sainct martin la contesse.
Et voyez son filz de grant noblesse
Leurs chevaliers et leurs heraulx.
    Et voyez en cest eschauffaulx
Le capitaine dudit conte
Ses chevaliers sont bien du compte.
    Voyez l'hermit en ce boys la,
Qui sainct martin batisera.
    Et voicy le pauvre nud
Qui par sainct martin sera revestu
    Voicy marmoustier et l'abbe
Et son secretain en arroy.
    Voicy l'homme qui se pendra
Et sa femme qu'il occira.
    Voicy ceulx qui fera dacord
Dequoy l'un deulx sera le mort.

Voicy Tours en cest estre icy;
L'archevesque y est aussi,
L'archediacre sans faillir,
Est avec luy pour le servir.
    Cy est le taillandier sa fille
Et sa femme sans nulle guise.
    Et aussi voicy par deca
Cil qui le vestement aura
Qui luy sera par trop petit.
    Cestuy qui a cest autre habit
Est un mesel trestout pourry,
Qui de martin sera guary.
    Le pape est la en ceste estre,
Qui est de l'eglise le maistre.
Son messager est devant luy
Qui fait les messages pour luy.
    Icy aussi est sainct Ambroyse
Et son cler vous pouez veoir.
    Voicy le clop et l'aveugle,
Guaris seront vueillent ou non vueillent.
Diables sont en enfer la-bas
Lucifer et les sathanas.

The objection may be raised that the word
là-bas does not necessarily mean " *down* there "
when applied in this play and in others to the
setting of Hell. Yet the word occurs very often
in lines referring to Hell, and is synonymous
with *en bas* (Greban, line 33488). Greban
uses the word *descendre* with it in line 12197:

et la-bas au limbe descende, while the phrase
lassus au limbe, even though in the unacted
prologue, shows Greban's idea of the level of
Hell proper. These expressions occur too often
to be merely rhetorical. The opposite expressions, *là-haut, en haut, monter* applied to
Heaven, are not found to be rhetorical. If the
prologue be read, one feels that the author by
beginning with Heaven *en haut* and ending his
enumeration with Hell *là-bas* (down there) has
wished to bring out the contrast between the
two scenes naming the highest, first, and the
lowest, last, in order. The place of Heaven can
admit of no discussion: *en hault* is exact. If
Hell were on the same level with the rest of the
stage why is *là-bas* used for Hell alone? Why
does the author not continue with *voicy, voilà,*
or *là* when he points out Hell unless he uses
là-bas meaning "down there"? The word can
hardly be ambiguous, used as it is, in this passage; and the prologue calls for three levels of
the stage. Also, judging from the way in which
the scenes are enumerated, we again have the
arrangement of the stage with Heaven at one
end and Hell at the other. The same plan is
used in the *Mystère des Trois Doms: et en*

*oultre au dessus y avoit paradis devers le levant
et enfer au cochant.*

All of the characters named in the prologue
did not have a *maison.* The directions and lines
of the play serve to give information left out
naturally in the prologue, because when it was
recited the scenery was before the audience and
the scenes only needed naming, not description.
The *Roy de Hongrie* had a *maison,* for Martin
sleeps there when he is crowned. Also the *duc
de Millan* speaks of his house, saying *Montez ça
hault, venez ceans.* Other houses are those of
the prince, the captain, and the pope. The city
of Tours was shown and one line mentions the
gate of Paris which is not among the scenes enumerated in the prologue. The hermit lives in a
wood as usual. There is a chapel and a *moustier,*
the latter scene being well constructed. There
is an altar in it. (*Icy s'en vont pres de l'autel.*)
At least one pillar supports its roof, for a direction reads *Lors s'en va apres elles a l'eglise derriere un pillier,* the word *eglise* evidently referring to the *moustier.* Near, and perhaps con-
nected with this scene of the *moustier* and forming a part of it, is the room of Martin which is
reached by steps. When the devil has rung in

order that Martin may be called to the *moustier,*
Martin starts *et en entrant aux degrez il tombe
du hault en bas.*   In commenting on this play,
Petit de Julleville says that nineteen different
scenes were represented at once.[2]   But even if
the gate of Paris be counted—it may have been
behind the scenes—and the *chambrette* of Martin
be reckoned as a separate scene, there are only
fourteen different scenes really set.   Not all
characters enumerated in the prologue had a
separate scene.

The *Vie de Saint Barbe* needed Heaven and
Hell; the *maison* for Marcian and his people;
maison of Dioscorus; *maison* of the four ty-
rants; a prison; *maison* of the *prévost;* two
chambres in which St. Barbe appears.   The
gibbet may be counted as a "property" rather
than as a scene, while the place of the messen-
gers and that of the beggars were probably not
decorated.   Thus there were nine scenes, one of
which at least was not on the same level with
the rest.[3]

Somewhat more complicated was the stage
for the representation of the *Vie de Saint Clé-*

[2] *Op. cit.,* vol. II, p. 536.

[3] Petit de Julleville counts eleven or twelve, *op. cit.,*
vol. II, p. 486.

ment, when the following scenes were set: the imperial palace and the Forum at Rome; the Alps; the *citadelle* of Élégie; a forest; an amphitheater before the Serpenoise Gate at Metz; palace of the governor; a tavern; another inn; a cemetery; Paradise and Hell. The Moselle Valley and the public square noted by Petit de Julleville[4] were probably on neutral ground.

This number is very much reduced, in turn, in the *Mystère de Saint Laurent*[5] in which there are eight scenes: Heaven and Hell, and six maisons. These indications are given in a prologue. The scenes are numbered and the text indicates all changes of scene.

The *Mystère de Saint Vincent* also explains the following scenes in its prologue: Heaven; Hell; Palace of Diocletian; Palace of Maximian; the Roman senate in the Capitol; Palace of Dacian; wood; Valence; *maison* of Valerian; temple; prison; boat.[6]

[4] *Op. cit.,* vol. II, p. 494.

[5] Acta Societatis scientiarum Fennicæ, vol. XVIII, p. 111. Published by Söderhjelm and Wallensköld.

[6] For Prologue see Cohen, *Histoire de la mise-en-scène,* pp. 76–77. Petit de Julleville adds one more scene—*maison des ensevelisseurs*—which was probably without decoration. *Op. cit.,* vol. II, p. 563.

These miracles differ little from the more complicated *Miracles de Notre Dame* in number and kind of scenes produced. Twelve scenes is about the highest number they reach, although one or two may have gone beyond this limit. There is this difference, however, that the *Miracles de Notre Dame* make little of the scene of Heaven, and Hell is very rarely shown, while in these plays, although Heaven is not as great a scene as in the Passion plays nor is Hell set so carefully, yet both of these scenes have grown in importance. The lack of directions in these plays, showing just how scenery was set, is again indicative of the fact that less attention was paid to their setting as a rule. Also, although the setting of Heaven and Hell did become important in the fifteenth century, there are plays even in this period and later in which these scenes do not appear at all or are unimportant. In *S. Bernard de Menthon*[7] Heaven is represented above the stage, but little of the action takes place in it, while Hell may not have been visible at all. When the devils enter they are directed to come *" de loing."* The scene of Hell, if set at all, was of practically no use to

[7] Soc. des ans. textes français, vol. 25.

the action. If the mystery of the *Siège d'Or-
léans* was played, no Hell scene added any
interest to the play, while in Paradise there
were only five characters: God, St. Michel,
Notre Dame, St. Euverte and St. Aignan. The
mystery of *S. Louis* by Gringore, produced
about 1514, contained neither a scene in Heaven
nor Hell, but required a stage of one level.
Even in plays dealing with the life of Christ,
such as the play of the *Nativité* reprinted in
the Silvestre collection, Hell is not visible. The
stable is shown, and the floor is covered with
straw. There is a pastoral scene. Heaven is
above the stage, but it is a scene of little importance. Excerpts from the larger Passion
Plays similar to this one must have been produced very often, and a stage would be set without the Hell scene. Therefore we must again
refrain from deciding upon the typical stage
of the period.

The mystery of the *Trois Doms*,[8] given at
Romans in 1509, was mounted with great care
for scenic effect. The stage was raised upon
pillars and stood in the courtyard of the con-

[8] Mystère des Trois Doms joué à Romans en MDIX.
Giraud. Lyon, 1888.

vent of the Cordeliers. It was *"36 pas ou 18
toises 3 de long et la moitié de ces dimensions de
large."*[9]   (The toise $= 1$ meter 949 mil. in
1789.)   The description of the stage is given
in part as follows, in the expense book:[10] *Et
samblablement sur ladicte platte form estoit
litelle entremy des villes, cités, comme Rome,
Vienne, Lion, et aultres et les sieges eslevés cellon
les personnages; et tous les jours change la sta-
tion cellon le mistere; et lequel clodis estoit
peynt tout en gris comme liteaulx et tours, et sur
ladicte platte forme estoit le premier jour tout
couvert de verdure, le second de fleurs de diverses coleurs le tiers de rozes; et en oultre au
dessus y avoit paradis devers le levant et enfer
au cochant.* This arrangement of scenery with
Heaven at one side of the stage has occurred so
often that it cannot be said that on the stage of
the Middle Ages Heaven dominates all.[11]   At
times, as has been shown, the scene in Heaven
demanded a large area; but also this setting
must be kept in mind where the scene was
placed merely at one end of the stage and on a
higher level.

[9] *Op. cit.,* p. xliv.
[10] *Op. cit.,* p. 592.
[11] Petit de Julleville, les Mystères, vol. I, pp. 388, 402.

There was more scenery than the *maisons* mentioned above as is learned from the following item in the expense book: *Item, plus seront tenus lesd. chapuys dedans lad. plate forme faire tours tournelles, chasteaulx, villes de boys.* . . . Thus the cities were not always summarily represented by the gate and wall as the famous Valenciennes miniature would lead one to believe; but the buildings were also shown, as is seen from the action and the stage directions. In Vienne, for instance, there is a scene in a theater: *S'en vont au theatre, et s'asiet sus les bans alentour.* In Rome there are *maisons* as well as the *porte de Rome* representing the city. At the same time the characters have their seats; and these and the rest of the scenery are changed from day to day *celon que le mistere le requerra.* Thus was the number of scenes kept down even on an open air stage.

Little can be known about the setting of Heaven in this play except that it opens and closes. Once a *petit Dieu* appears in the middle of a sun. Hell is entered through a dragon's head. (*Entre dedans enfert tous, et puis la gueule se clost . . . Sortira par l'oreille destre d'enfert.*) The interior of Hell is none the less open to view for Proserpine speaks *sans se bouger d'enfert,* and naturally a character who is speaking is seen by the audience. What part then does the dragon's head play in this setting and in others of which it forms a part? Is it the entrance to the regions in Hell where action takes place; or does it serve as an exit; and when the devils passed through it were they lost to view? Petit de Julleville says: *Le premier plan de la scène . . . recouvrait et cachait l'enfer, et lui ouvrait un passage par une trappe cachée derrière un rideau, qui representait une tête hideuse et grimaçante. . . .* (les Mystères, vol. 1, p. 388.) But the interior of Hell was visible to the spectators in many plays as we have been careful to prove; and such an arrangement would not permit the action to be seen which was carried on within Hell. Probably the scene was set so that the devil, in going to the side of the stage where Hell was supposed to be, would reach the dragon's head and would pass through it and be still in view of the audience during the scenes in Hell. The dragon's head would therefore face the stage, not the spectators. If the jaws formed a real exit, a trap through which the devils went, the setting

12

could not be considered as an entrance to that
part of the Hell scene visible to the spectators;
but it was merely an entrance to the depths of
Hell, the *parfont,* which was thus hidden from
view but from which smoke, and noise, and
devils arose. The dragon's head may have
" hidden and covered" a part of Hell in this
manner, but did not shut out the whole of
Hell from view.

Roy, in reconstructing the setting of Hell in
the *Jour du jugement*[12] by aid of the miniatures, places the dragon's jaws at the left of
the theater behind which there is a wall with
barred openings and a gate. But why are there
two gates of Hell, one exterior, the other interior? The action does not demand two. If
there were two, it would seem more probable
that the dragon's jaws were in the interior.
Their presence could then be explained by the
fact that they served as an apparent entrance
to the depths and a real exit for the devils. But
Roy is trying to explain the two representations
of the entrance of Hell in the miniatures by the
possibility of both gates and jaws having been
shown on the stage. This confusion is rather

[12] Le Jour du jugement. Publié par Roy. Paris, 1902.

due to the artist who read the word *gueule* in the manuscript and drew one; then, later—and who knows how much later—he read the word *portes* describing the entrance of Hell and drew them.   Perhaps he had forgotten about the *gueule;* perhaps he wished to vary his illustrations.   At any rate we must not feel called upon to explain the different turns of the imagination of the artists.

The *Vie de S. Didier*,[13] played at Langres in 1482, is an example of a play which required the setting of Hell in the form of a dragon's head and nothing more.   There is no scene in Hell.   The devils swarm out of it on the stage. The tortures which take place within are "messengered."   The *gueule d'enfer* here plays the rôle of a mere exit which has been so often ascribed to it.   The *diablerie* is a diverting part of the action; but the setting of Hell is not designed to arouse great interest.   There is nothing in the text of the play nor in the stage directions to indicate that Heaven was either richly or carefully set.   The scenic display was centered in one locality, the city of Langres. The prologue reads in part as follows:

[13] Vie et passion de monseigneur Sainct Didier.   Guillaume Flamang.   Paris, 1855.

Véez là Lengres, en hault assise,
Plus noble que tous aultres lieux;
Véez là les seigneurs de l'Eglise
Et les borgeoys jeunes et vieulx.
Véez là Didier au labourage,
Qui tient la cherrue à deux mains;
Véez là ung haultain personnage,
Nommé l'empereur des Romains;
Croscus et le roy des Alains
Ont illec leurs gens amassez;
Je n'en diray ne plus ne mains;
Le demeurant se monstre assez.

The other settings which were so easily recognizable were Heaven and Hell. The city of Arles appears as a location, but does not appear to have been marked by special scenery. In the Third Day, Paris is mentioned: *Car vesci Paris la cité;* but as this scene is not needed until the latter part of the play, it would not be set until later. Thus the prologue is silent concerning it.

The setting of Langres is one of the remarkable scenes of the Middle Ages. Here is no mere gate to represent a city, but a city itself in miniature. One of the characters describes it:

Voylà le lieu d'antiquité,
Les tours, les portes et l'église.

This is by no means rhetorical, for the towers, the gates, and the church are needed by the action and must have been shown. The church contained an altar, and later the tomb of Didier. Also the pulpit, over which a cloth is spread when Didier preaches, is probably in the church. The city is surrounded by walls large enough to contain the citizens when they are besieged. The tower upon which the guard stands contains a clock. (*Les Bourgeoys . . . s'en vont sur les murs; la Guette monte en une tourelle où il y aura une cloche.*) The gate of the city can be closed. All this was set upon scenery representing "dark-colored rock" (*roche bise*). As the prologue tells us, the city was above the rest of the stage, and, as the lines indicate, had the appearance of being on a high mountain. (*Sur la haulte montaigne assise.*) Yet even with this realistic setting, chairs are still used by the characters. (*Icy les bourgeoys et le bailli de Lengres se lèvent de leurs sièges. . . .*) Rome itself seems to have no other setting than the throne of Honorius.

The siege of Langres was very life-like. When the barbarians arrive there is a pause in the lines in order that they may make their besieging works. (*Pausa pour faire le parc.*) The battle is carried on as follows: *Adonc tirent aucunes serpentines ou couleuvrines et ceulx de Lengres gectent pierres et aultres traits. . . . Lors est le feu bonté en ladite Ville.* The interior and exterior of the city must have been visible at the same time, and this would be arranged by removing the wall toward the audience. Since the barons are summoned from one place, as is plainly seen by the action, although they are supposed to hold different chateaus, all of the set scenes have been described above. They are few; but the scene of Langres shows a great advance in the representation of a city.

A stage upon which neither Heaven nor Hell was represented served for the *Vie de S. Louis* by Gringore. Thus the stage sometimes consisted of but one level even in the religious plays. As for the rest of the setting it was very simple. The play is divided into several "books" each of which was perhaps given separately. Five or six well-known scenes, such as a church, a palace, a wood, etc., serve usually for each act. In the seventh book there is a palace, a wood, executioners, fire and pillar, and an abbey. The setting for the action of the eleventh book required a mill, a river, the monastery of St. Denis, a ditch. The latter was well enough constructed to carry out the direction: *Icy tombe la terre sur eulx.*

There are then many kinds of stages for miracle plays. As far as levels are concerned, we find settings on one, two, and three levels. As a rule Heaven and Hell are of less importance in these plays and do not seem to have been as carefully set as in plays dealing with the life of Christ. There are two distinct settings for Hell. In the one, the dragon's head served as a mere exit and the interior of Hell was not shown; in the other, the interior of Hell was visible and the dragon's head was either an entrance into Hell or an exit into an imaginary part of Hell. It is difficult to say which of these rôles the dragon's head fulfilled. Also in some of the plays the entrance to the visible part of Hell was no doubt figured by gates. It is erroneous to believe that the dragon's head always appeared, and that it alone represented Hell.

One of the greatest spectacles was the representation of the *Actes des Apôtres* which began at Bourges on April 30th, 1536, and lasted for forty days. The whole town aided in the presentation of this play, which demanded five hundred actors and which was mounted in an ancient Roman amphitheater. The list of properties and machines[14] has been preserved and furnishes many interesting details in regard to the performance. The scenery itself does not seem to have differed from that of contemporary plays given in the open air. Heaven and Hell were both represented and there were the usual *maisons.* The scenery was changed to suit the action no doubt, as was the general rule, from day to day and not merely from book to book of the play as Petit de Julleville implies.

Paradise opens and closes: . . . *par ouverture des cieulx et aparicion de Jhesuscrist séant à la dextre de son père.* A vessel descends from Paradise full of all kinds of beasts and then returns. Another clever machine is described as follows: *Fault qu'il soit envoyé de paradis jusques sur led. monument une nue ronde en forme de couronne où aye plusieurs anges faincts tenant en leurs mains espées nues et*

---

[14] Le Mystère des apôtres représenté à Bourges en avril 1536. A. de Girardot. Paris, Didron, 1854.

dards, et fault s'il est possible qu'il y en ait de vifs pour chanter.

The light effects are carefully noted: *et fault que en lad. prison apparoisse grande lumière.* At another time there descends upon the Cenacle *du feu en espèces de langues avec clarté.* Again the face of St. Etienne appears *luisant comme le soleil.*

There are trap doors, for the devils come from below earth in the form of dogs; and another direction reads: *Fault que St. Mathieu soit mis soubz terre en lieu où il puisse aller par dessoubz se mectre au mailleu de Ephigenie.* . . .

Many temples with idols are represented, as for example: *Fault ung temple en Suanier, et en iccelluy à costé dextre doit avoir ung chariot d'or tiré à beufz, et dessus une lune, et du costé senestre ung autre tiré à chevaulx et dessus ung soleil d'or.* One of the other temples collapses on the stage.

Maisons are used as is customary: *Fault ung hostel pour St. Pierre qui soit paré avec une chaire où il sera comme tenant le siège apostolique.* Thus the *chaire* alone did not represent the scene. Another *maison* is in the form of a *haute tour faicte en forme de capitole sur laquelle montera Symon Magus pour voller, et y doit venir une nue collisse, à demy ronde, pour l'eslever en l'air.* . . . A very unusual scene is that of the *siège paré en l'air près Paradis pour Justice divine.*

The ship which takes St. Paul to Rome bears *coffres et autre mesnage pour gecter en la mer de la navire et fault que le matz de la navire se rompe en deux pièces.* The steering of the ship is accomplished by a *polye au matz et une cheville en terre, et passer une corde en lad. polye pour virer lad. navire.* Once the sea gives forth its dead for a moment: *Doit venir sur l'eaue plusieurs autres corps mors agitez des vagues qui se pourront retirer soubz terre quant temps sera.*

The machines for this production were quite remarkable. The stage decoration was perhaps the most interesting part of the whole representation. Neither pains nor time nor money was spared by the town of Bourges to make the spectacle a success. With it, we leave the open air mystery, this wonderful combination of pageant and drama—drama in the wider sense

—and we turn to the inclosed theater. It is to be hoped that these great scenic displays have not been described at such length as to cause one to overrate their importance in the development of stage decoration.

CHAPTER XI

The Indoor Stage at Paris. Dimensions of Stages. The Question of Two Rows of Scenes on Separate Elevations. Setting of the *Vieil Testament*. Number of Scenes Set at One Time. Heaven and Hell Not the Most Important Scenes.

In beginning his discussion of stage decoration, Morice said: "It is not in Paris that the stage decoration must be studied in order to form a just idea of it. There, the *confrères* enclosed in the four walls of a building never had anything but a circumscribed theater and a cramped stage. It is in the magnificent representations executed in the principal provincial towns and which sometimes necessitated whole years of preparation . . . it is there that one must transport himself in imagination in order to seize the vast workings of this strange spectacle in all its development."[1] This point of view has been too often taken because the great

[1] Morice, Histoire de la mise-en-scène depuis les mystères jusqu'au Cid, p. 32.

spectacles are more curious and because there is more information to be had concerning their setting. Although Paris was not so completely the center of dramatic art as it became later, yet when we consider the inclosed stage of the *Puy de Notre Dame,* which is believed to have been near the *Hôpital de la Trinité,* and the inclosed stage of the *confrèrie* placed in the *Hôpital de la Trinité,* then transferred first to the *Hôtel de Flanders* and finally to the *Hôtel de Bourgogne* which Corneille and Molière visited, is not the inclosed stage at least as important in the history of the French theater, if not more important, than the out-door stage? The religious and profane plays alike are produced within a permanent theater. Whatever influence the drama of the Middle Ages may have exerted upon later French drama, the most of it must have come through the *Hôtel de Bourgogne* and not from the irregular performances of plays in the open air.

What, then, were the conditions which existed in these theaters, for theaters they are in every sense of the word? What was the size of their stage in comparison with the out-door stage? How did plays demanding such scenery

as did the *Actes des Apôtres* and the *Vieil
Testament* admit of production on any small
stage? All these questions cannot be answered
with entire accuracy and satisfaction; but a
general idea of these stages may be built up.

The out-door stage could be very large. Yet
its dimensions were by no means limitless, for
the audience had to see the action even if the
hearing of the lines was not indispensable. The
stage at Rouen was 60 meters long.[2] This must
have been more or less impracticable as far as
the spectators were concerned. Large theaters
are spoken of as having been erected at Metz in
1437, at Vienne in 1510, at Autun in 1516,
while *Actes des Apôtres* had the roominess of
an amphitheater in which to spread out its
scenes. The largest theater, at least as far as
seating capacity was concerned, was the theater
erected at Autun in 1516.[3] However, the stage,
which was 60 meters in length, was undoubtedly
considered as extraordinarily spacious even in
the Middle Ages. As has been shown, the number of *maisons* set upon this stage at Rouen
was larger than the usual number required at

[2] Cohen, *op. cit.*, p. 87.
[3] Petit de Julleville, *op. cit.*, vol. 1, p. 405.

one time. The stage of the Trois Doms erected
at Romans was about 35 meters long and half
as wide.[4] These figures may probably be accepted as the average size of the out-door stage
when a whole town was backing the enterprise
financially. A somewhat smaller stage was one
which measured 19 meters 50 by 4 meters 90.[5]
These temporary stages naturally varied greatly
in size according to the play which was to be
produced and the amount of money to be spent
on the representation.

The measurements of the *Hôpital de la
Trinité* were 6 × 21½ *toises*[6] or somewhat less
than 12 by 42 meters. The *Hôtel de Bourgogne* was built on a space of 16 × 17 *toises*[7]
in size or about 31 by 33 meters. The stage
and audience room together of the permanent
theaters were about the size of an open-air stage
of average dimensions. The narrowness of the
first of these halls precludes the possibility of a
stage running lengthwise, for if room for
scenery and neutral ground be allowed on such

[4] See p. 174.

[5] Cohen, *op. cit.*, p. 83.

[6] Petit de Julleville, *op. cit.*, vol. 1, p. 420.

[7] Recueil des principaux titres concernant l'acquisition
de . . . l'hostel de bourgoyne. Paris, 1632, p. 31.

a stage there would be little room for spectators.
The stage, then, may be conceived as occupying
one end of the hall. It was therefore not quite
12 meters across. Its depth is a matter for
conjecture. Perhaps we are not far wrong in
allowing five or six meters. The stage of the
Hôtel de Flandres which the *confrérie* occupied from 1539 to 1543 was probably of similar
dimensions. It was in this theater that the
Actes des Apôtres and the *Vieil Testament* were
produced.

The in-door stage presented a very different
appearance from the stage of the amphitheater
set for the *Actes des Apôtres*. There were
fewer scenes set at the same time within the
theater. Much of the splendor of the scenery
must have been lost, and no doubt some of the
machines were impracticable in so small space
as was offered by any of these theaters. The
mounting of these plays, however, was perfectly
possible, and it must not be supposed that the
scenery was more or less chaotic. It has already
been shown that parts of plays could be cut
out at will.[8] The manuscript of the mystery
of *Saint Genis* also indicates passages which

[8] See p. 86.

were not given during a representation.[9] As
scenery could be changed from day to day in
the out-door productions, so it was changed in
the theaters. The length of the performance
was from one to five in the afternoon.[10] Thus
the part of the play given in this length of time
would not demand, as a general rule, very many
different scenes. Cohen is of the opinion that
the scenes were set on two levels in the inclosed
theater, some of them forming a second story.
It is thus that he explains the directions found
in the *Vieil Testament* such as: *If fault que
icy soit Joseph descendu et assis en chaire, non
pas au parc du roy mais ailleurs.*[11] Pharaoh is
seated *en hault* and also the doctors. Cohen
publishes a miniature of Jean Fouquet showing
a second story of a stage in which is found
Paradise, the emperor, certain devils and some
spectators. The question is a delicate one to
decide, and Cohen has strong evidence in favor
of his theory. Yet the procedure is strange in
view of the realistic method of stage setting in
vogue, which separated the levels so carefully.

[9] Petit de Julleville, *op. cit.*, vol. II, p. 521.
[10] Cohen, *op. cit.*, p. 86 ff.
[11] Sec p. 91.

13

Similar directions have already been found in some of the early plays of the Jubinal collection;[11] and the conclusion was reached that this arrangement may have been employed to raise certain characters in their chairs or scenes above the stage so that they might be more easily seen. The *Histoire de S. Louis* also shows the scenery raised above the stage in this manner by such directions as: *Tous montent en hault; Le conte de Provence monte en haut; Il vont à la royne Blanche sans descendre.* Thus while a few steps may have led up to this scenery which was raised in order to be better seen, there is no evidence that it formed a second story, and that other scenes were set directly under it. Is it not such an arrangement which Jean Fouquet has attempted to reproduce in the miniature? The Hell's mouth is below the rest of the scenery. The torture takes place on neutral ground. Heaven is on one side of the stage; Hell is on the other. At the rear, and raised, is the emperor's throne. Why is Heaven not shown above all? Perhaps the artist was inaccurate. Perhaps the fact that Heaven was above the neutral ground was sufficient for the demands of realism.

[11] See p. 91.

That the scenery was raised at the rear of the stage seems to be an established fact. It may be that the sloping stage, which is the rule in French theaters to-day, is due to this custom. But it is difficult to admit that there were two stories of scenes supposed to be on Earth, the one superimposed upon the other.

In producing the *Vieil Testament* the *confrérie* had little trouble. It easily divided itself into parts or " acts " which would fill the time allotted to the performance. The part which deals with the creation was the most elaborate from the point of view of scenic effect; but the setting which is required is quite possible on the stage of the *confrérie*. It was more effective in light effects. In imagining the setting one must reduce the dimensions of the scenes, and one must realize that fewer scenes are set.

When the action opens, God is in Paradise, above the stage as usual. *Adonc se doit tirer ung ciel de couleur de feu auquel sera escript: Celum empireum.* The Angels enter: *Lucifer ayant ung grant soleil resplandissant darriére lui.* God is seated on high in Heaven, for when Lucifer tries to reach his lofty throne, *Lassus en haulte eternité* (line 285), a rubric directs the action thus: *Adoncques se doivent eslever Lucifer et ses Anges par une roue secrétement faicte dessus ung pivos a vis.* Lucifer and his angels fall; and the devils, who are "ready in Hell," make an uproar and throw forth jets of flame. Whether a dragon's head served as entrance or not, the interior of Hell was visible, and there follows a scene within it, as the following lines show: *Car je suis au parfont du puis* (line 518); *Sommes au parfont d'Enfer fondus* (line 530). These expressions and others such as *en ce gouffre* point to a scene at least below Paradise and Terrestrial Paradise.

The creation of the world is shown almost entirely by scenery. God descends from Paradise with his angels. *Adoncques se doibt monstrer ung drap peinct, c'est assavoir, la moityé toute blanche et l'autre toute noire.*[12] This is the separation of light from darkness. *Adoncques se doit monstrer comme une mer, qui par avant ayt esté couverte, et des poissons dedans*

[12] Cohen, *op. cit.*, p. 159, believes that this direction shows how darkness was represented when called for by such rubrics as *Icy font les tenebres*. But while this serves as an excellent allegorical representation of the separation of light and darkness, it is a question whether the lowering of a black cloth showed nightfall.

icelle mer. Unfortunately the means by which the sea was represented are not described. The scene was ready beforehand, but was hidden from view. Its disclosure meant the creation of water. Perhaps cloth was used for the setting as it is to-day. The creation of plants and trees was realistically represented. *Adoncques doit on faire sortir petis arbres, rainseaulx et le plus de belles fleurs, selon la saison, qu'il sera possible.* The sun, moon, and stars arise. *Adoncques doit on faire monstrer un grant soleil. Adoncques se doit monstrer la lune plus bas que le soleil. Adoncques se doit monstrer ung ciel painct, tout semé d'estoilles et les noms des planettes.*

Terrestrial Paradise is also disclosed, it evidently having been hidden from view until it was supposed to have been created. *Adoncques se doit monstrer ung beau Paradis terrestre, le mieulx et triumphamment fait qu'il sera possible et bien garny de toutes fleurs, arbres, fruictz et autres plaisances, et au meillieu l'arbre de vie, plus excellent que tous les autres.* This scene has a gate as is learned from a later direction: *Icy est Cherubin sur la porte de Paradis terrestre.* The scene is further described: *Adoncques se doivent monstrer quatre ruysseau, comme à maniére de petites fontaines, lesquelles soient aux quatre parties du Paradis terrestre et chacun d'iceulx escrips et ordonnez selon le texte.*

If the *Confrères* represented this part alone in one afternoon, which is quite possible, it is seen that their stage would present a quite different appearance from the stage of an out-door mystery, set for the action of a whole day which sometimes embraced over 10,000 lines. Such a stage as the one described would be very different from the stage of the *Nativité* at Rouen in 1474. In fact this setting resembles a modern setting in extent, more than the regular out-door stage. Even if the scenes were given up to that of the flood—more than this could not possibly be produced in four hours— the only settings to be added are a " city; " (*Icy font une cyté Enoch, Yrard et Lameth*); a house for Cain (*Méne moy en la maison,* line 4875) and a very simple out-door scene in a field or wood (*Il m'est advis qu'en ce buisson . . .* line 4743). The *couche pour coucher Eve* and the *fosse* for Adam are not exactly separate scenes. A natural division, however, would be made after the Creation and the Fall of man. Taking into consideration that the action and representation of the Creation would require so much time, it is probable that the play stopped after the *Procès de Paradis* and began the next day after the Fall.

A new setting is needed for the flood. The ark is shown and is entered. *Icy entrent Noé, sa femme et ses enfans en l'arche, et y mettent plusieurs bestes et oyseaux de differentes sortes.* Since there are scenes within the ark, its interior must have been made visible probably by means of opening the side toward the audience. The flood is realistic. *Icy surmonteront les eaues tout le lieu, la ou l'en joue le mistére, et y pourra avoir plusieurs hommes et femmes qui feront semblant d'eulx noyer, qui ne parleront point.* Finally it ceases to rain. We are hardly to believe that the *eaues* were real. Although a scene has already been noted in which real water is supposed to have been used,[13] such a scene as the one described above would be impossible unless the water was merely represented. After the cessation of the flood an altar is built, the rainbow appears, and the tower of Babel is erected.

[13] See p. 142.

A break then occurs in action, and probably the performance ended there to begin anew the next day.   One of the most complicated settings is demanded in chapter XVI., which was probably represented on the second day, following the one described above.   The house of Lot appears; a tabernacle is mentioned by the lines; there is a tree; and finally comes a direction: *Icy fondent les cinq cités.*   Yet this is not too much to set even on the in-door stage, although the number of scenes set could probably not exceed six or seven.   Six scenes is the average number in Hardy's plays produced at the *Hôtel de Bourgogne.*[14]   Day after day the stage must have been set with fewer scenes, since the lines which could be played in four hours often do not need more than three or four.

Also, day after day the action does not demand any scene in Heaven or Hell.   The result is that the audiences of the Middle Ages were accustomed to a view of a stage which had very few scenes, and was on one level, and on which Heaven and Hell were not always shown even in religious plays.   The scaffolding for

[14] Rigal, Théâtre français avant la période classique. Paris, 1901, ch. VI.

Heaven was probably permanent; but we can hardly believe that the scene was always set and occupied by characters who had nothing to do with the action. As for the setting of Hell, it was surely removed when the action did not need it, if for no other reason than to make room for other scenery. We cannot say, therefore, that Heaven and Hell were the most important scenes even on the religious stage of the Middle Ages. When one pictures in his imagination the stage of this period, if he only sees a platform of great length, with many scenes, surmounted by a scene in Heaven, and with a dragon's head at one end, he is far from realizing the whole truth in regard to this very changeable and elastic theater.

CHAPTER XII

The Profane Stage Setting of the *Maulvais Riche*.
Setting of *Moralités*.   The *Sottie*.   The *Farce*.

THE *Enfants sans souci* and the *Basochiens*
made an arrangement by which each could use
the repertory of the other. This gave the *Basochiens* the right to play *sotties* as well as *moralités*. Their stage was the famous *Table de
Marbre* in the Palais. It is reported to have
been 40 meters long by 12 meters 70 wide.
Thus their stage was large enough for the
scenery demanded by almost any play. On the
other hand the *Enfants sans souci* joined with
the *Confrères* and thus brought the profane
pieces on the stages of the *Trinité,* the *Hôtel de
Flandres,* and the *Hôtel de Bourgogne.* There
were also representations in the open air of profane as well as religious plays. The problem of
the difference between the setting of the inclosed
and open stages of the purely comic theater is
not one of vital import, since scenery is much

less complicated in the farces and *sotties* than in the miracle and mystery plays.

No strict line of demarcation can be drawn between the religious and profane drama. The two kinds mingle in morality plays, miracles, and *histoires*.[1] Thus it is with their setting. The general rule that scenery which was necessary to the action was set, holds good for all kinds of plays. One might make a distinction between the two kinds of plays on the ground that most religious dramas are set on a stage of at least two levels, the higher of which is occupied by Heaven, while the purely profane drama rarely represents Heaven. The Hell scene, however, appears in the comic stage in the *Farce du Munyer,* and in the morality of *Bien Avisé et Mal Avisé.* In the latter play, Hell is described as a kitchen: *Devez noter qu'il doit estre en manière de cuisine comme cheuz un Seigneur, et doit illec avoir serviteurs à la mode. Et là doit on faire grant tempeste*

---

[1] In treating the different kinds of drama the classification made by Petit de Julleville has been followed. Thus plays treated in his work entitled *les Mystères* have been considered as religious, while the examples of the profane theater have been taken from his *Répertoire du théâtre comique au moyen âge.*

*et les ames doivent fort crier en quelque lieu
que l'on ne les voie point. . . . Adonc chacun
face son office et boutent et frappent sur la table
d'ung baston, et devez sçavoir que la table doit
être noire et la nappe peinte de rouge.* After
the guests are served a sulphurous meal, the
devils force them into the depths of Hell which
were covered by the dragon's head. Thus we
have an example of a stage on which there was
a scene in Hell open to view, and on which the
dragon's head appeared, although the play cannot be called religious. Yet the influence of the
setting of religious plays upon that of the profane plays is clearly shown. No doubt when
the farces, which were produced on the stages
of the *Confrères,* needed scenery, the *maisons*
which served in the religious plays were utilized. For this reason, namely, that scenery was
already waiting for the farces in the inclosed
theaters, it is to be believed that every scene
in comedies produced in these theaters was as
carefully set as the scenes in such plays as the
Passion, even though stage directions in the
manuscripts of farces and *sotties* are very rare
and by no means explicit. Again the lines
must furnish the information concerning the
appearance of the stage set for comedy.

The *Vie et l'histoire du Maulvais Riche*[2] is a play which represents Heaven and Hell, although it can hardly be classed as religious drama except from the point of view of stage decoration. The situation of the Heaven scene is above the stage, for *Dieu le Père* says: *Pour ce te convient devaller là-bas.* There are long scenes in Hell before Lucifer, and a part of the furnishing of the place is a cauldron in which a soul is tortured. There is no mention of a dragon's head, however, as being used either for entrance or exit of the scene. The house of the *Maulvais Riche* was carefully set. There were two rooms one of which was a kitchen: *Tout droit m'en vois en la cuisine.* The other room served as a dining room. A table is set and the meal is brought. Although the door is closed— *Trotemenu, ferme la porte*—the interior of the house was still visible. There was also a window represented: *Que je vois en celle fenestre.* This play holds the middle ground between the two styles of stage decoration. It has the Heaven of the religious drama; but the

[2] Fournier, Théâtre français avant la Renaissance. Paris. Viollet-le-Duc, Ancien théâtre français (Bibl. elzév.).

little scenery on Earth—in this case but one *maison*—is a characteristic of the profane stage, notwithstanding the fact that in the productions of purely religious drama in-doors there were often few scenes set.

Moralities without a scene in Heaven or Hell are the most common. In the *Moralité nouvelle contenant comment Envie au temps de Maintenant*,[3] etc., stage directions furnish indications for most of the simple scenery such as: *Pause, et vont les premier et second filz sur la verdure, où ilz se couchent;* and *Ilz le jectent en la cyterne.* The *verdure* must not be considered as rhetorical when referred to by a rubric. In addition to this scenery the lines show a house: *Partez-vous tost de la maison.*

Two moralities which show the same simplicity of stage setting are the *Moralité d'ung Empereur qui tua son nepveu*,[4] etc., and the *Moralité . . . d'une Femme qui avoit voulu trahir la cité de Romme.*[5] The former only requires two scenes. The emperor is *En sa chambre.* The house of the maiden does not

---

[3] Viollet-le-Duc, *op. cit.*

[4] Viollet-le-Duc, *op. cit.*

[5] *Ibid.*

seem to have appeared on the stage; but after she is abducted she is spoken of as being *en ceste chambre là*. This is all the scenery that is necessary; and the rest of the action passed on neutral ground. The latter play requires the interior of a prison as its only set scene. The house of the daughter is behind the scenes, and the three Romans seem to have merely occupied chairs in giving their judgment.

In the *Moralité de Charité*[6] a prologue, instead of naming the different scenes, points out the characters who are on the stage with the exception of *Mort,* who is *en une ruelle* or, in other words, behind the scenes. This change in the function of the prologue is a natural one in view of the fact that there was practically no scenery to explain. The only scenery on the stage was that of the house of the *riche avaricieulx* and the house of the *riche vertueux.* The references in the lines to these houses are born out by the direction: *Elle entre,* which shows *Charité* entering the house of the latter. A table is also set within this house. The characters speak of a tavern; but as they never really arrive at it the scene was surely not set.

[6] *Ibid.*

One of the most famous moralities is that written by Nicolas de la Chesnaye, the doctor of Louis XII., entitled *Comdamnacion de Bancquet.*[7] It is supposed that this play was in the repertory of the *Enfants sans souci;*[8] thus it was given at the *Hôpital de la Trinité.* The characters sit down as they do in the mysteries when their part is temporarily finished. The doctor opens the play. Then comes the direction: *Après ces motz, se retirera le Docteur et se yra seoir jusques à ce qu'il viendra faire son sermon.* Another influence of the religious theater is seen in the orchestra which is *sur l'eschaffault ou en quelque lieu plus hault.* This latter place is undoubtedly that part of the stage where the scene in Heaven was set in religious plays and the organ or orchestra was stationed.

The first scene takes place at the house of *Bonne Compaignie* where a repast is served either on a "round or square table." *Disner* takes *Bonne Compaignie* and her followers to his house which he points out plainly:

> Veez cy mon logis et demaine;
> Veez cy l'éstat tout preparé.

[7] Jacob, Recueil des farces, sotties, et moralités du XVe siècle, p. 273.

[8] *Ibid.*, p. 270.

There are two tables in the house, one for the guests, and a serving table. (*Le Cuysinier aura ses metz tous prestz sur quelque autre table et les baillera aux servans.*) The house is not merely represented by the tables, but has walls and windows. (*Notez que Soupper et Bancquet les espient par quelques fenestre haulte.*) The house of *Soupper,* where the next repast is held, also is provided with a window, as is proved by a direction similar to this one just cited. The kitchen is also shown, for *Soupper* carries out the action implied in the lines:

> Je voys visiter le quartier
> De la cuysine cy auprès.

The cook points out the many dishes which are prepared. The third meal takes place at the house of *Bancquet.* The house of *Experience* is merely marked by a chair: *Experience, dame honnestement habillée, sera assise en siege magnifique.* A prison is also called for by the rubric: *Clistere les maine en prison.* A gallows completes the scene.

Gringore's morality[9] needs practically no scenery. The references of *Peuple Ytalique*

[9] Gringore, Œuvres (Bibl. elzév.), p. 244.

14

and of *Peuple François* to *maisons* do not appear to point to scenery set upon the stage. *Pugnicion Divine* is, however, *hault assise en une chaire, et elevée en l'air,* so careful were the dramatic authors to see that the scenery carried the ideas set forth in the play. This play, belonging as it did to the *Enfants sans souci,* was produced in the *Hôpital de la Trinité.* The chair of *Pugnicion Divine,* therefore, would be placed on the level which served for the scene in Heaven.

There is, then, no general type of stage which can be assigned to the morality. Its stage at times resembles that of the mysteries and shows scenes in Heaven, in Hell, and on Earth. There is also the setting which shows Earth and a scene in Hell, while the *Comdamnacion de Bancquet* requires neither a scene in Heaven nor one in Hell. Finally there is the morality which demands no setting whatsoever but depended upon lines and costumes to arouse interest. Examples of this class are *Moralité Nouvelle de Mundus, Caro, Demonia,* and *Marchebeau.* The *Bergerie de mieulx que devant* merely had one setting of a pastoral scene.

Scenery is unimportant in these plays when there is little action and when the subject is of a satirical nature treated allegorically. When there is a real plot and action, however, as in the *Comdamnacion de Bancquet,* even though the subject is allegorical, scenery is generally required. Its function is more to explain the action than to arouse the wonder and admiration of the spectators. When compared with other moralities, *Bien Avisé et Mal Avisé* seems to be rather an exception in this respect, with its evidently elaborate Hell scene and its revolving Wheel of Fortune to which four men are attached who are named respectively: *Regnabo, Regno, Regnavi, Sum sine regno.* The *Moralité de l'homme juste et de l'homme mondain* also had a careful setting. Its stage must have resembled that of a mystery play, especially in the setting of Heaven. *Est à noter que Paradis sera faict au costé des Cieulx un peu assez loin. Et dans ledict paradis y aura la Trinité, Nostre Dame et les saincts suivant leur ordre.*[9a] The influence of the stage decoration of the religious drama on the setting of the morality play is again very plain. Yet, though these spectacular

[9a] Frères Parfaict, vol. III, p. 120.

scenes exist, the morality cannot be considered as being primarily a spectacular production. Scenery generally plays a secondary part in the representations of this kind of drama.

The *sottie* resembles the shorter allegorical moralities in the matter of stage decoration. Settings are sometimes entirely lacking as in the *Sottie du Monde*[10] and the *Sottie des Béguins*.[11] In Gringore's *Jeu du Prince des Sotz*[12] there is a direction: *Il descend* given to the *Seigneur de la Lune*. Thus the character probably came down from a moon; but there is no scene which is formally set. The *Sottie nouvelle de l'Astrologue*[13] is merely a political satire in dialogue. It is, therefore, without action and without scenery.

There must have been a simple setting for the *Sottie du Roy des Sots*[14] which conformed to the following dialogue:

Sottinet.
Je voy ung fol par ce pertuys.

[10] Fournier, *op. cit.*
[11] *Ibid.*
[12] Gringore, *op. cit.*, p. 201.
[13] Société des anciens textes français, vol. 47.
[14] Viollet-le-Duc, *op. cit.*

Le Roy des Sots.
Où? où?
Sottinet.
Au dessus de cet huys.

Guippelin is then dragged forth from this implied *maison;* no other decoration seems to have appeared.

One scene was probably set for the *Sottie des Trompeurs.*[15] It was a house in which *Sottie* is found; and it is implied in the line in which *Fine Mine* says of *Sottie: Je l'ay veue par la fenestre.* This might be considered as being rhetorical were it not for *Chascun* saying: *Ouvrez,* to those who are supposed to be within the house. *Teste Verte* also says: *Ferons-nous Chascun entrer ceans?*

An allegorical scene was set for the *Sottie du Vieux Monde.* First there appeared six trees from each one of which a *sot* came forth. The world, in the shape of a large pasteboard globe, was raised upon six pillars, which, in turn rested upon a table called *Confusion.*[16] The structure falls during the play.

The stage decoration of the *sottie* in general

[15] *Ibid.*
[16] Morice, *op. cit.,* p. 273.   Frères Parfaict, *op. cit.,* vol. II, p. 230.

was very meager. Of all kinds of theatrical
representations in the Middle Ages, this one
lends itself least to any setting. Again it is
the nature of the play—a dialogue with little
action—which seems to be the cause of the lack
of scenery. Costumes, in a measure, took its
place.

The farce shows many gradations of stage
setting. Many plays of this kind were given
without any setting, such as: *Mestier et Mar-
chandise*,[17] *Farce de Folconduit*,[18] *Farce de
Jolyet*,[19] etc. The art of stage decoration, however, is so far advanced by the time that the
extant farces make their appearance that the
fact that some require decoration and others do
not, proves nothing. We cannot say that there
was an evolution of stage setting in the farces.
It is true that the early farce of Eustache Des-
champs, *le Dit des .1111. Offices* is without indication of or reference to scenery; but it is not
because of the early period of production, for
stage decoration was, of course, a well-known
art in the middle of the fourteenth century.

[17] Fournier, *op. cit.*
[18] *Ibid.*
[19] Viollet-le-Duc, *op. cit.*

We also find farces of the sixteenth century without scenery, such as the *Farce des Theologastres.*[20] The existence or non-existence of scenery depends not upon the time of the production of the farce, but, as in the morality, upon the nature of the plot. If there is much action there is generally some scenery.

A very simple setting occurs in the monologue of the *Franc Archer du Baignolet*[21] in which the direction is found: *Il doit avoir un espovantail de chanevière en facon d'un arbalestrier, croix blanche devant et croix noire derrière.* The *Farce du Cuvier*[22] must have given the stage the appearance of being set for an interior, but for only one scene. The washtub, into which the wife falls, appeared on the stage. What other properties there were, we cannot say. A single scene within a house was also necessary for the *Farce d'ung Savetier.*[23] during the action of which a table is set in an interior (*Or vous seez donc à la table*). In the *Farce nouvelle du Nouveau marie*[24] the scene

[20] Fournier, *op. cit.*
[21] Viollet-le-Duc, *op. cit.*
[22] *Ibid.*
[23] Fournier, *op. cit.*
[24] Viollet-le-Duc, *op. cit.*

opens at the house of the father who tells his daughter: *Entre, tu soys la bien venue.* They are about to have supper. Here, again, the setting is that of an interior; and this is the only scene possible. A similar interior is implied in the *Farce de Jeninot*[25] in the direction: *en se couchant dedans un lict.* Only one scene is required by the *Farce d'un Pardonneur, Triacleur, et d'une Tavernière.*[26] This is a tavern, into which the actors enter. (*Venez, entrez, j'ay de bon vin.*) A *chasteau* is the setting for *Folle Bobance.*[27] It is pointed out by the line: *Entrez, vella vostre demeure.* Of course the exterior of some of these scenes was shown, as in the *Farce de frère Guillebert*[28] which requires an interior with a bed, while an actor who was visible out of doors speaks the line: *Et puis, hay, m'ouvrirez-vous l'huys?* Such settings, however, may be considered as consisting of but one scene.

The *Farce de Colin*[29] is one of the very few plays of this kind which contains information

[25] Viollet-le-Duc, *op. cit.*
[26] Viollet-le-Duc, *op. cit.*
[27] *Ibid.*
[28] *Ibid.*
[29] *Ibid.*

in regard to setting in its stage directions. There is a bench (*La Femme s'assiet sur ung banc en plourant*); and also the interior and exterior of Colin's house, for Colin *va en sa maison, et dit en entrant.* The setting of the interior must have been very complete, for a direction reads: *Il se met a table;* and the lines point to the following objects:

> Et ce beau lict, ciel et cortines,
> Simaises, potz, casses, bassines.
>
> . . . .
>
> Bancz, treteaux, tables, escabelles.

The setting of an interior of a house, with the exterior so often visible as well, is quite a common setting on the stage of the Middle Ages by virtue of these farces.

An example of a stage set with two scenes is found in the *Farce du bon payeur.*[30] The house of Lucas into which *Vert Gallant* enters is necessary to the action and is shown by the line: *Sa femme qui file à son huys.* The *payeur* is found in bed in his house. (*Est il heure de se lever?*)

The *Farce du Munyer*[31] also has but two

[30] Fournier, *op. cit.*
[31] *Ibid.*

scenes: the house of the miller and a scene in Hell. This farce was given in Seurre in 1496 on a stage set for a representation of the *Mystere de saint Martin* composed by André de la Vigne, who is also author of the farce. It was during the representation of this mystery that the accident took place which is reported as follows: . . . *celuy qui jouoit le personnaige de Sathan ainsi qu'il volut sortir de son secret par dessoubz terre, le feu prist à son habit autour des fesses, tellement qu'il fut fort bruslé.* The Hell scene in the mystery was, therefore, sufficiently realistic; and no doubt the farce used the same scene. The interior of Hell is proved to have been visible by the direction in the farce: *Icy la scène est en Enfer.* A cauldron forms one of the properties of this scene. (*Ilz lui apportent une chauldière.* The house of the miller is mentioned in the direction: *Le curé, devant la maison.* The miller is within, *couché en ung lict.* . . .

In *Pathelin*[32] there are three scenes. First, there is the house of Pathelin, in which there is a bed. That there is really a house and not merely a bed on the stage is shown by the direc-

[32] Jacob, *op. cit.*

tion: *Il frappe à la porte de Pathelin.* The second scene is the shop of the *drappier* shown by the direction: *devant la boutique du drappier.* Pathelin enters the shop and sits down. Thus the scenery was no mere summary representation of the place. Finally there is the scene before the judge who was probably seated in a chair; but there seems to be no other setting for this scene.

In regard to the construction of scenery, Rigal has a theory which may well be considered in the light of these plays. He says: *Pour les habitations, la nécessité d'une telle convention était plus grande encore, parce que là plupart des cabanes, des ermitages, des chambres, faisaient face, non au public, mais à la scène. Il était impossible d'y faire dialoguer les acteurs; tout un côté de la salle ne les eût point vus, et l'autre côté lui-même aurait eu de la peine à les entendre. Que faisait-on? Si la chambre renfermait "un lit bien paré," un personnage pouvait se montrer d'abord sur ce lit, qui occupait le point le plus en vue du compartiment; mais il s'en levait bien vite, et venait parler hors de sa chambre. La plupart du temps, c'était sur le seuil même des chambres,*

*des ermitages, des cabanes, que les personnages
se montraient, et ils ne s'y tenaient même pas.*[33]
If this is true, Pathelin would go to bed and
show himself for a moment, then rise quickly
and come out of his room to speak.   The miller
would do the same in the *Farce du Munyer*.
He would not die in bed, as he manifestly does.
Such an action would spoil entirely the cleverly
built situation of Pathelin feigning illness in
bed and it would have become, under these conditions, unintelligible to the audience.   Rigal
does not give any source for his belief that it
was the side wall of the *maisons* which was
taken out.   Such a proceeding would be impracticable, and would seem to cause unnecessary difficulty.   Therefore, just as the artist of
miniatures in the Middle Ages left out the wall
of the *maison* which faces the eyes in order to
allow what was going on within to be seen, so
the stage carpenter surely left out the front wall
of his *maisons*.   This is the obvious and sim-
plest way of showing an interior.   Doors and
windows were then in the side wall, which was
foreshortened enough to allow a full view of the
stage.   This is the plan which is followed at the

[33] Rigal, *op. cit.*, p. 264.

present time if two rooms or an exterior and interior must be visible simultaneously on the stage.

Farces which require more than two settings are rare, yet the *Farce du Poulier*[34] probably used four scenes. The miller's house is required by the lines:

> . . . Je mettray
> L'huys hors des gons, si tu ne m'ouvre.

The hen-house is also shown. (*Cachez vous dedans ce poulier.*) There is also a house for Mme. de la Papillonière implied by the line: *Il ne vous desplait pas si j'entre.* There is nothing in the text which refers to a house for Mme. la Hannetonneur; but since she plays a similar rôle to Mme. de la Papillonière she had some sort of a *maison,* in all probability, in which she was visited. The hen-house was, in reality, a part of the miller's house, for the two gallants, when concealed in the hen-house, can see what is going on in the miller's dwelling. In another farce[35] on the same subject the chicken coop is in a second story, as is shown

[34] Mabille, Choix de Farces, Nice, 1875, vol. II, p. 94.
[35] Mabille, *op. cit.*

by the words: *montez au poulier*. Perhaps this arrangement existed in this play, for the gallants may well be looking down from above, rather than through a door or window placed so that the interior of the house is visible from their hiding place. This setting, then, really consists of only one important scene and two minor ones.

The stage when set for a farce had little scenery. This style of dramatic representation was very popular during the fifteenth and sixteenth centuries. Therefore the stage of the Middle Ages was often very simply decorated. In the farce, Heaven was never represented, and Hell was rarely seen. The stage often consisted of but one level. The scenes were set simultaneously in purely profane drama; but they were few in number in comparison with the religious drama, and they were far less elaborate. The Parisian, therefore, was quite accustomed, after 1402, to a stage with few scenes and on one level. This stage is just as characteristic of the Middle Ages as the large temporary platform on which many scenes were placed including Heaven and Hell. In fact the Parisian may have considered the great open air spectacles, as we consider performances in a Hippodrome[36] or on the large stage of an opera, as being out of the ordinary in regard to scenery; while the *Hôpital de la Trinité* and *Hôtel de Bourgogne* with their small stages may have seemed to him to constitute the regular and normal theater from the beginning of the fifteenth century when the inclosed stage was established permanently.

[36] We refer to the New York theater of that

CONCLUSION

THE existence of liturgical drama was the result of an attempt to make certain religious ceremonies more real and life-like. In order to heighten the effect of reality the altar was considered as representing the sepulchre or the manger. Such scenes are primitive beginnings of a system of stage decoration which lasted through many centuries. Do we find this the spontaneous and unconscious origin of modern stage setting? Did the people of the Middle Ages suddenly awake to find that the Church had created drama and had introduced scenery? If it be granted that drama was introduced into the Church from profane shows of some kind, the question of the origin of scenery is still unanswered. It would be possible for the dramatic form of art to live without scenery, yet the element of setting was so important in the earliest medieval dramas, which have been preserved, that it is easy to believe in a figurative, summary setting in profane mimes. Thus as we accept the theory of an unbroken dramatic tradition, so we accept the theory of an unbroken tradition of stage decoration, although we realize the futility of attempting to prove that this was the case from data available at present. It is merely the impression which has arisen during the study of the whole question.

Whatever setting there was during the period of attempted suppression of dramatic performances by the Church, and during the rise of religious drama, was undoubtedly improvised and much must have been left to the imagination. Proof of this is found in the description of the earliest settings which are known to us. The liturgical drama, however, soon spread out its field of action. As the play grew more complicated, so the scenery followed it. A play was written in which the action occurred in two places. The scenery representing them was set before the action began and the simultaneous stage setting existed. This may have happened in either the religious or profane drama. The first extant example of this system occurs in religious drama.

The liturgical drama discards makeshift and improvised scenery, and uses real scenery,

15

finally. Its scenes are set on one level. The
Hell scene is shown very rarely, and there is
no setting which formally represents Heaven.
These two scenes are the least important of all
in this kind of drama.

The custom of setting the scene in Heaven on
a higher level is foreshadowed in the liturgical
dramas in which angels appear from on high;
and, in the *Adam* play, Terrestrial Paradise is
placed on a level above the stage. A Hell scene
is also indicated in this play, although probably the entrance was the only visible part of
the setting, and there is little reason for conjecturing that the scene was in the form of a
dragon's head as early as the thirteenth century.
Had this setting been popular so early, it is
not probable that it would have been considered
as something wonderful in the fifteenth century.

The stage of the thirteenth century is set
with few scenes. There seems to be hesitation
between the stage of one level and that of two
levels. There is thus little difference between
the appearance of the stage set for religious
plays and one set for profane representations.
There is a development in the importance of

scenery, which begins to fulfill the function of adding interest to the production as well as of making the action clear. This secondary use of scenery to delight the eye grows in importance when the plays in pantomime and tableaux are represented along the streets.

In the latter part of the fourteenth and the beginning of the fifteenth century dramatic productions must be divided into two classes: those given in-doors and hence on a small stage, and those given in the open air on stages built to meet all demands of the play in regard to scenery.

Productions in the open air were no novelty even in the thirteenth century; but the mimed productions of the fourteenth and fifteenth centuries must have influenced these representations in the matter of stage decoration. The fact that no word was spoken in these pantomimes and tableaux would force the setting to be exact and interesting. The people grew accustomed to a long, out-door stage upon which there were many places represented with elaborate scenery. It is but a short step to the great spoken mystery in a market place or an amphitheater. The step is made by having the char-

acters speak.   On these stages the setting
reached its highest point of development.
Heaven and Hell were very important scenes
and were set with great care.   The stage showed
two and three levels and sometimes more, as in
Michel's version of the *Passion*.   The number
of levels often depended upon whether the interior of Hell had to be open to view or not.
These productions are very wonderful and
curious, but they are more or less of an episode
in the history of the French drama.   They
reached a certain point in their development
and then disappeared, with the exception of a
few scattered performances in later centuries.
No doubt the existence of such spectacles in the
open air tended to make the scenery of the indoor stage more realistic; but these two kinds
of stages must have differed, not in principle,
but in result.

The indoor stage is smaller.   There are few
scenes set upon it.   This is just as true in 1636
as in 1402.   Religious and profane dramas were
given on these stages.   The Parisian saw many
kinds of stage decoration; but he was fully accustomed to a small stage with few scenes.   The
question of whether Heaven and Hell were

shown or not depended upon the play.   A stage was often set without either scene or sometimes with one and not the other.

It was this setting of five or six scenes which Hardy used and of which Scudéry said in 1637: *Le théâtre en est si mal entendu qu'un même lieu représentant l'appartement du roi, celui de l'infant, la maison de Chimène et la rue presque sans changer de face, le spectateur ne sait, le plus souvent, où sont les acteurs.*   In the *Trois Sosies,* Rotrou uses the same words which occur in the mystery plays in the direction: *le ciel s'ouvre.*   But this system of stage decoration was destined to fall into disuse with the advent of the three unities.

The method of setting several scenes at once upon a stage ought to need no apology.   At first glance one is likely to consider this system as naïve.   But all drama rests upon convention. Perhaps no other form of art demands such a complete surrender of the reasoning power to the imagination and so perfect an understanding between the producer and the recipient. One may easily believe a story no matter how extravagant it may be; but in the theater everything is a sham and unreal.   At present we are very free in regard to theatrical conventions. The supernatural may be introduced on the stage in any form. One will believe that years have intervened, or that thousands of miles have been traversed, provided a curtain is dropped or the theater is darkened for a moment. The medieval spectator did not need this aid to the imagination. He could turn his eyes from one scene to another without being awakened from his delightful unreal world. At times the dramatic effect was even heightened by the exposure of different scenes at once. Imagine for a moment the dramatic contrast in seeing the blessed in Heaven and the damned in Hell at the same time. Who shall say that this system is any more naïve than the one in vogue at present! If the audience of the Middle Ages did not wish to let their eyes wander, there was practically but one scene before them at a time; and the spectator was not called back periodically to the garish reality of a theater as he is in modern times.